"Killed at Saarbruck!"

"Killed at Saarbruck!"
A British Newspaperman's View of the Franco-Prussian War

Edward Legge

"Killed at Saarbruck!"
A British Newspaperman's View of the Franco-Prussian War
by Edward Legge

First published under the title
"Killed at Saarbruck!"

Leonaur is an imprint of Oakpast Ltd
Copyright in this form © 2011 Oakpast Ltd

ISBN: 978-0-85706-791-3 (hardcover)
ISBN: 978-0-85706-792-0 (softcover)

http://www.leonaur.com

Publisher's Notes

The views expressed in this book are not necessarily those of the publisher.

Contents

From London to Cologne	9
Going to the Frontier	13
Coblenz	17
The Preliminary Movements	21
Under Fire for the First Time	28
In Search of a Legitimation	33
At Cologne Again	42
After the Battle	46
En Route to the Front	50
Scenes in the Hospitals	54
An Escape from Saarbrucken	58
The Bombardment of Toul	64
From Commercy to Clermont	69
An Alarm at Buzancy	75
A Days Rest at Raucourt	79
After Sedan	86
An Awkward Position	96

The author, upon his return to England,
was not a little surprised at being shown the following,
which appeared during his absence
in the London papers
as a telegram from the seat of war:—

> "I regret to announce the death of one of my colleagues. Herr Legge, Special Correspondent of the ———, was shot through the head at Saarbrucken on the 2nd of August. I received the news from two English officers."—*From the War Correspondence of the* VIENNA OLD PRESS, *August*, 1870.

Chapter 1

From London to Cologne

The war between France and Prussia, which was officially declared on the 18th of July, 1870, brought into requisition the services of a host of gentlemen, who, appointed to record in the newspapers the movements of the armies for the benefit of the public, lost no time in getting to the scene of hostilities. I received my commission to act as Special Correspondent for ———— on the 23rd of July, almost a week after the declaration of the war; and on the 25th of that month I left Charing Cross railway station for Dover, having first obtained a Foreign-office passport—a document absolutely necessary those troubled times.

It was a hot summer, morning when I drove to the station through the quiet London streets. The sun shone from a sea of blue sky; the perfume of the flowers in Convent Garden Market was wafted by the light breeze into the Strand; the platform of the station was crowded with people waiting for the departure of the Continental train; and, as I entered a carriage with my arms and pockets full of newspapers, I pondered upon the appearance of the stations at Cologne, at Coblentz, at Bingen, and at Mayence, that glorious morning.

My destination was the headquarters of the Prussian army, wheresoever they might be; the route primarily being Dover, Calais, Brussels, Cologne. There was no excitement *en voyage* to Brussels, The beach at Dover was dotted by a few loungers who had strolled down to see the Calais and Ostend boats start;

and I found Calais as dull and picturesque as ever. There were the same fishing-boats moored alongside the quay, the same sentinels pacing up and down the ramparts, the same broken-English-speaking gentry at the railway station; but as to war, or preparations for war, nothing was to be seen. In some of the shop windows were highly-coloured caricatures of Count Bismarck, and others representing Prussian soldiers in positions of great abasement; and when I walked round the market-place I was greeted by a group of small boys with the cry, "*A bas le Prusse!*" though I was no more a Prussian than an Otaheitan or Ojibbeway Indian. The hotels were empty, all the visitors having left in view of the coming conflict; and the proprietors spent their days and nights in lamenting their hard fate, and execrating those who had caused the war.

I reached Brussels in the evening, and found the old Belgian capital *en fête*; it was the Festival of Saint Somebody, and the streets were decked with flags and triumphal arches, and all were taking their pleasure.

Nothing like war so far.

On the platform of the railway station I encountered a gentleman who announced himself as the correspondent of a London evening paper.

"I suppose you, like myself, are hurrying to the front?" I observed. "When do you expect to catch up the army?"

"No," he replied; "I am not so ambitious as that. I shall be satisfied if I can get to Cologne."

"But you will see nothing there," I ventured to remark.

"Oh yes," he answered. "Cologne is full of soldiers; great excitement; proper place to go to; can't do better, I assure you."

On the following morning I left Brussels for Cologne, and, as the incidents *en route* were noteworthy, inasmuch as they brought me *en face* with I portion of the German armies, I transcribe from my note-book some of the most interesting.

It was after leaving the junction station of Verviers that I saw the preliminaries of war. At Verviers you leave France and Belgium behind, and get on Prussian territory. The mail carriages display the eagle of King William's country, every signal-post and telegraph-pole is painted black and white, and you hear for the first time during the journey the full, guttural German words shouted by strong-lunged guards and porters. Immediately after leaving Verviers, its handsome *buffet* crowded with travellers, amongst whom were many English, fortifications cut in the solid rock, which extends for a long distance to the left of the railway, and big guns, just showing their noses through the loopholes, compete for admiration with a very English-looking country—cuttings bedecked with wild flowers common in Berkshire and Surrey; meadow lands of which a Lincolnshire yeoman might well be proud; and pine forests whose gloomy shadows only serve to bring up more distinctly the beauties of the landscape.

At Aachen I saw "first blood" drawn by a Frenchman. There is excellent raspberry brandy to be had at Aachen station; of this a Frenchman and a Prussian had gotten too much, and at the end of their potations they fought with patriotic ardour for twenty minutes, until the Prussian, whose nose was bloody, and whose eyes were of the hue of the sloe, gave in amid the jeers of his fellows. A quarter of an hour after leaving Aachen we came upon a sight which made all our hearts beat quicker, for it was the uprising of the curtain behind which preparations were making for the great drama of War! Drawn up a short distance from the railway was a squadron of Prussian Hussars—splendid fellows, in blue uniform, and admirably mounted.

At the next station we stopped parallel with a train full of troops, and the spectacle so affected a pretty *fraulein* in our carriage that she leaned out of the window and waved her handkerchief excitedly to the *soldaten*, who in turn cheered her lustily. The *fraulein's* eyes were wet with tears when she sat down, and she was particularly engaged for the next hour in reading a *zeitung*, which completely hid her face. Between Aachen and Cologne there was the greatest excitement, for we were now fairly in a country whose inhabitants were in the midst of war preparations. Gliding quickly by a factory town where there is a veritable bit of black country scenery, reminding one of Wolverhampton or Dudley, we pull up at Eschweiler, to find ourselves surrounded by soldiers, who are almost concealed in an immense cloud of tobacco smoke, for everybody smokes in Germany, save the priests, who would also *fumée* if they dared to.

A strange scene, and a characteristic one. Fritz has his arms round Wilhelm's neck, and is bidding him cheer up; several village girls have come to the station to see their sweethearts off; even the good clergyman of the place is there amongst the men, whom, as children, he christened; and who, if they be so lucky as to escape the bullet, and shrapnel, and grenade of the *Fransozens*, will return to their beloved birthplace, to die, perchance, at a green old age, and be buried with their fathers in the little churchyard where the tall grass waves mournfully over many a grave marked by the plain cross which is common to both Catholic and Lutheran. On the other side of the line, in a train crowded with soldiers, they are singing "*Die Wacht am Rhein!*" and you could imagine them going anywhere but to the war!

Chapter 2

Going to the Frontier

I found Cologne station thronged with soldiers, and the good townsfolk suffering from a sharp attack of war fever. They apprehended an onslaught upon their city. The French were at Forbach, and there was a rumour that they intended to march to Cologne, or sail down the Rhine in their gunboats! Preparations were at once made to defend the town. The fortifications were inspected and ordered to be increased; the lumbering old cannon were cleaned and generally furbished up; the trees around the city walls were all cut down, so that they might not interfere with the cannon fire when the enemy should arrive; and it was even feared that the beautiful public gardens would have to be despoiled, and the charming country houses in the suburbs destroyed, on account of the hindrance which they would offer to the cannonade from inside the walls.

Nothing but war was talked about. In a very practical way the inhabitants set about their self-imposed task of assisting the *soldaten*, and providing them with provisions and cigars. Every train brought in thousands of spiked-helmeted, blue-tuniced men, all a-hungered and athirst after their long journey. Ladies and gentlemen—professional men and shopkeepers—all who had a few *thalers* to bestow upon the defenders of the Fatherland—waited the arrival of the soldier-trains; waited with baskets choking with *butter-brod, kase, schinken,* red wine, and cigars; and when the trains came in it was marvellous how quickly all these good things we disposed of. They have tremendous appetites, the German *soldaten*, and their capacity for drinking is illimitable.

I am afraid to guess at the quantity of *schnapps*, and wine, and beer, imbibed by them daily on their way to the frontier; and as to the number of cigars, and the amount of *tabac* they smoked—that would require the ability of the calculating boy to solve!

Besides the townspeople, the students who get their preparatory education at Cologne, before passing through the more severe *curriculum* at Bonn, Kehl, Jena, Heidelberg, and Leipzic, threw their books on one side, and hastened to place their services at the disposal of the town authorities, for the distribution of food to the soldiers. Subscriptions for purchasing lint and other necessaries were opened, and the *Salle Gurzenich* (concert saloon) was converted into a "Lazareth," for the reception of the wounded. This was something more than sentiment, a quality of which the Germans are said to possess an undue amount; it was the kindling of that patriotic flame which once lighted, never went out, and which carried the armies of Germany successfully to Paris.

The news that the Germans residing in London had subscribed 100,000 *thalers* (equal to £15,000 sterling) in aid of the wounded was received at Cologne with great satisfaction, and men went from *restauration* to *restauration* proclaiming the good news. Wednesday, the 27th of July, was observed throughout Germany as a day of prayer and thanksgiving for the victory which the Prussians had already obtained at Saarbrucken on the previous Saturday, when the French were repulsed. There was a special celebration of the Mass at Cologne Cathedral at nine a.m., and I was a spectator of the thanksgiving service. The grand old Dom was filled with military and civilian worshippers. It was an awe-inspiring scene, and one which fixes itself in the memory.

The magnificent church; its many columns, which, with the rich carving and tracery, are like the work of fairy architects; the altar, with its huge candles, flowers, and statuettes; the richly-robed priests; the acolytes in long red cassocks and white surplices; the citizens, their wives, and handsome flaxen-haired daughters; the simple-minded *fraus* in neat white caps, and hair plaited with exceeding neatness; the children praying before the statues of the Virgin; the little flower-decked space near the choir; the deep diapason of the organ, thundering through the vast space; the melodious voice of the officiating priest; and above all the intonation of that mass of soldiery, praying to the God of battles to send them victory—this was a spectacle which thrilled all hearts!

Looking around at the *cuirassiers* in their gay uniforms, and the *landwehr*, sombrely clad, all kneeling side by side that summer morning, expecting at any moment to hear the roll of the drum, and the trumpet-call to arms, made me ask myself the question, "When the war is over, and the peace-day festival comes, how many these boy-warriors will answer to the roll?" When next I saw them, it was on the battlefield at Saarbrucken, and Beaumont, and Sedan, maimed, bleeding, dying, or dead!

Leaving the Dom, I found the people making holiday after mass, as the custom is; the street were full of all classes, who eagerly read the news posted on the walls; the *cafés* were crowded, an resounded with patriotic songs; the newspaper offices were surrounded; and all were bent upon anything but business. At this time Cologne was in a state of siege, and all the gates were strongly guarded. Down by the Bridge of Boats, and that other handsome bridge over the Rhine, steamers and large sailing boats, full of hay, straw, wheat and oats, were making all speed up the river to Coblenz and Mayence, whither most of the stores were being dispatched.

Many of the steamers carried soldiers and horses; others were weighed down to the water's-edge by the large pieces of artillery which they had on board; and there was no cessation of their movements upstream. On the quay all was bustle and excitement. People came down to see their friends off, and nothing but farewells and the "*vorwarts!*" of the officers and *fitzwebels* (*sous officièrs*) were heard. Soldiers hurried down the steps and across barges to reach the steamers, and the air was black with the smoke from twenty funnels. As the boats steamed slowly upwards, the people on shore and those on board made the place ring with their cheers and songs; and ere many hours had elapsed I found myself and my knapsack on one of these same craft, gliding over the waters of the Rhine through a dense mist and up a steady rain.

Chapter 3

Coblenz

The Rhine is an Epic—the Moselle is an Idyll." An "Epic" I certainly thought it as we steamed up the noble river in the *Prinzessin von Preussen*, on the 27th of July, two days after I left London bound for the Prussian headquarters Prussian soldiers lined both sides of the "sacred stream," as the Germans fondly call it; the blue tunic and helmet of the Prussians were everywhere sometimes we saw them on the bank, and sometimes from the window of a little tavern, where Hans, and Karl, and Ludwig were quartered. The Father of Rivers was no longer the resort of the tourist-world, but bore on his broad breast the brown faced, light-haired, blue-eyed men, burning with impatience to be led against the *Fransozens* who had declared that they would have Berlin, and that the *Emperor* should sign the peace at Königsberg!

At nine o'clock, seeing some lights in the distance, I asked the steward, who, I fear, had taken too much Strasburg beer on the voyage, "*Ist das Coblenz?*" and he answered me thickly, and with the salt tears of inebriety in his red eyes, "*Jah, mein Herr. Das ist Coblenz.*" There were 30,000 men quartered there; but I declare the quiet which prevailed would have done credit to Pompeii or the buried city of Herculaneum. The Firmungatrasse was empty—the Parade Platz silent as the grave! And yet there were 30,000 soldiers in the town! It was like being in a city of the dead, and I felt ashamed of myself for keeping such late hours. There was nothing to read in the *salle-à-manger* of the "Aulser" but a *Kölnischer Zeitung* a week old, the last number but one of *Kladderadatsch*, and a copy of the *Daily Telegraph*, beer-stained and torn, but brought to me nevertheless by the waiter with a smile all over his face.

It was impossible to sleep when I got to my bedchamber, so I looked out of the open window at the great fortress of Ehrenbreitstein, opposite, the construction of which cost five million *thalers*. Only a solitary light showed where the fortifications stood; on the bridge of boats a few lamps flickered; all else was in shadow; and the yellow waters of the Rhine gurgled musically and mournfully under the boats. I have only just succeeded in closing my eyes when a noise on the quay arouses me; it is four o'clock, and I gaze upon an extraordinary scene. There is a thick fog, not black, like an Irish fog, nor yellow like a London one, but a fog of the hue of burnt sienna, enshrouding everything in its dim embrace.

Through this opaque mass of cloud and mist I see two steamers, having many men on board; the steamers are the *Goethe* and the *Schiller*, and the men on board are Prussian soldiers, whose destination is "up the Rhine"—to Mayence, in fact, whither I followed them. Not without some difficulty, however, for, in order to bring the troops from Castel, the Prussians had thrown pontoon bridges over the Rhine, near Mayence, just below the handsome stone bridge. This impeded the river traffic. All the soldiers were being dispatched to the frontier in the south. Train after train, steamer after steamer, teeming with men, baggage, and artillery, were destined for that point, where it was believed the enemy would make an attack.

As I am in the spacious *salle-à-manger* of the English hotel in the Rheinischer Strasse, my only companion a Prussian officer, the music of a military band announces some new arrivals, and through the crowded *strasse* marches the 6th regiment, the band playing that stirring melody of which the refrain is "*Ich bin ein Preussen!*" one of the most popular of the *soldaten-lied*. There was no limit to the transport of troops, thousands of whom marched through the country by night, that their movements might not be observed. No one could fail to be impressed with the appearance German soldiers——that I was so will be see from the following extract from my diary, written at Mayence. "I like the look of the Prussians very much. They are soldiers, every inch of them, and I know they will fight to the death. The best of it (or the worst of it, shall I say?) is that five out of ten do not know for what they are going to fight! In reply to my questions to several of them today as to what was the cause of the war. they said. 'They did not know; they were fighting for the King!' and '*For King and country*' is the motto which these *schnapps*-loving soldiers had written on their pipes,"

At Mayence there was extraordinary enthusiasm. Those who have been up the Rhine thus far will have seen that the railway runs all along the Rhine-strasse. This thoroughfare was the great attraction for the people of Mayence during the early weeks of the war; for along it passed at every hour of the day and night soldier-trains crowded with their living freights. Only a few people were privileged to pass through the entrance-gate. Amongst them were the wine and beer vendors, and those persons who had brought cakes, bread, wine, tobacco, and cigars for the troops, to whom all extended the right hand of fellowship.

The soldiers had as usual decorated the carriages with boughs of trees, and sang and looked as if they were a party of London excursionists going to the Derby or to Hampton Races, and not to give the enemy battle. They quaffed the red wine and the lager-beer from large jugs, and it was nothing but a chorus of "*prost!*" There was none of those sad *adieux* with which we became familiar in England during the Crimean war-time; for most of the men had come from distant parts of Germany, and had bidden their friends farewell at many a wayside station. But there was plenty of hand-kissing to the pretty *frauleins*, whose hair was fastened by those formidable-looking combs which you see in this part of the country.

On many carriages the men had written chalk "By express to Paris!" the humour of which sentiment no one failed to appreciate. A battalion arrived every hour from Castel, crossing the pontoon bridges, and marching down the Rhinestrasse to the station. A more enlivening and exhilarating sight it would be difficult to imagine than a battalion of *cuirassiers*, in all the panoply and pomp of war, marching through the Rhinestrasse at Mayence, led by mounted officers, followed by the band, the brass-topped helmets and the swords gleaming in the sun; the sparkling waters of the Rhine on one side, and every window filled by spectators. One battalion marched through the *strasse* with their band playing the melody of their own and our National Anthem; and the reader will easily conceive the delight with which English ears heard the grand old tune played in a foreign town in war-time, first by a regimental brass band and then by drums and fifes,

The town itself was so full of troops that it was difficult to move about in the principal thoroughfares. The Markt Platz, in which is the statue of Guttenberg, the father of the art of printing, offered a wonderfully picturesque sight during this period of the campaign. The countrywomen in their white caps, the soldiers in every variety of uniform, the large square a moving mass of humanity, the grand old cathedral looming over all, made a charming picture. The booksellers' windows were full of war literature, *Krieg-Karten* predominating over everything; whilst many shops displayed humorous caricatures of the Fransozens, not the least amusing of winch were those which represented the Enemy of Man carrying Napoleon in his arms, and exclaiming, "This is my beloved son, whom I hold with pleasure!" These were the *mauvaise plaisanteries* in which the German artists indulged, with which the people were satiated before the fighting had really commenced.

Chapter 4

The Preliminary Movements

Mayence was a general rendezvous. In the early days of the war everyone was to be found there. It was the centre of military operations. Prince Friedrich Karl resided at the house of the governor for several days at the beginning of August, whilst the German armies were being mobilized. The king subsequently had his headquarters in the town. As a passage for the troops, the Rhine, especially that part of it between Mayence and Bingerbruck, was invaluable. The soldiers crossed the river by three bridges—by the handsome stone bridge, by the famous bridge of boats, and by the pontoon bridge, which was thrown over for the purpose. And yet there were not more bridges than were required. From morning till night you heard the tramp of armed men, the rumble of the artillery carriages, the steps of horses crossing from Castel. All these troops were sent into the interior of the country without loss of time. Some went to the frontier—Saarlouis and Saarbrucken; others to Frankfort; a few to Saxony.

During a war the German soldiers are billeted upon private individuals—not, as in England, exclusively upon innkeepers. And the rich, as is but proper, bear the heaviest burdens in this matter. The higher a man's income is, the more men the Government sends to his house to be provided with beds and food. For this accommodation not a *pfennig* is paid. I have known instances of 100 soldiers being quartered on the premises of one gentleman! An American lady residing at Darmstadt, with whom I came up the Rhine, told me that her husband had had that large number of men sent to his house to provide with everything. The *soldaten* are not particulary agreeable visitors, but the *désagrémens* are overlooked by the Germans in their patriotism.

Naturally anxious to get to "the front," to which every correspondent was ordered, I stayed only one night at Mayence. My difficulties began from the moment I applied for a ticket to Saarbrucken. The clerk at the railway told me it was impossible to get to the frontier town. I replied that others had succeeded in reaching Saarbrucken, and that I had resolved upon doing as they had done. The official gave me a ticket to Bingerbruck, and I took my seat in a train full of soldiers. At Bingerbruck I saw the preparations which were being made for the campaign. A vast bakery was course of erection. All along the line were herds of oxen. Rhine steamers brought cargoes of hay and straw. Troops were constantly arriving at the junction station. A regiment of Bruswickers—the officers splendidly mounted—marched off towards the frontier a few minutes after our train reached the station. This regiment was one of the first on the march, and great interest was manifested as it moved off with its band playing, and the men singing.

As a matter of course, the railway traffic was much impeded—often, in fact, altogether stopped—by the exigencies of the period. The soldier-trains blocked up the line everywhere. Luckily there was a train leaving for Saarbrucken in two hours after my arrival at Bingerbruck, and in that I found a seat. We were soon speeding towards the frontier town through the valley of the Nahe—as charming in many places as the scenery on the banks of the Rhine. The railway runs for some distance at the foot of vineyards, laid out on the steepest of hillsides, with huge masses of rock and stone at their base. On the other side of the railway is the river Nahe, which runs by the side of forests and through a delightful pastoral district.

On wooded mountain-tops you get glimpses of flocks of sheep, herds of oxen, droves of pigs, goats, tended by some old herdsman with crook and dog. Perched high up on the mountains are the peasants' cottages—rude huts, with one room for the family, and an adjoining apartment tenanted by the cow, the sheep, the pig, and the goat. At all the stopping-stations the villagers with not a few ladies and gentlemen, came to meet the train, bringing baskets of provisions and bottles of wine and beer for the soldiers.

At Oberstein, a charming little town standing at the base of the mountains, with its church built on the solid rock, the distributors of the viands included several young ladies, whose faces glowed with the excitement of the occasion. There was much hand-kissing and waving of helmets and handkerchiefs as the train departed; and at the next station the scene was repeated. Greater kindness it would have been impossible to evince. The soldiers lacked nothing.

Between Otweiler and Saarbrucken the aspect of the country undergoes a striking change. You leave behind the quiet pastoral districts and enter upon a new land—the black country of Germany. The district abounds in minerals. There are iron factories and coal mines, and the river Saar and the railway are the channels for distributing the wealth of the district. Passing the blazing furnaces in the night, as I did, was not unlike going through a bit of our own marvellous Black Country—not unlike a ride through Wolverhampton and Dudley when the fires are lit and the air is full of flame and smoke.

It was nearly eleven o'clock that night ere we reached St. Johann, the suburb of Saarbrucken, and all the hotels were closed. I succeeded in getting a bed at an hotel near the station; but I had hardly closed my eyes when there was a rap at the door, and a servant came in with a request that I would permit some officers who were below to look at my papers. I sent down my passport and my card, and in a few minutes received the Foreign-office document with the thanks of the gentlemen who had perused it.

Saarbrucken has played such an important part in this terrible war that I cannot refrain from making some mention of it. St. Johann and Saarbrucken are two towns situated close to the frontier, divided by the river Saar, the waters of which have the peculiarity of changing their colour from brown to red, and from red to a dull neutral tint. St. Johann (the suburb to Saarbrucken) contains many houses built of the local stone, and will probably, at no distant date, be a fashionable resort. Its sister town is by far the oldest of the two places. The streets are irregular, the buildings have no pretensions to architectural beauty, and the town would be dull to a degree were it not for the presence of the military, for whose accommodation there are three barracks, portions of one of which were devoted during the war to hospital purposes.

The Saar in peace times is full of trading vessels, the traffic in minerals being very considerable; but when I saw it at the beginning of August it was a veritable "silent highway," with not a boat on its surface, A quarter of an hour's walk from the bridge which separates the two towns is Bellevue, where the first of the real fighting took place. From Bellevue you get one of the most charming prospects in Germany and France. The two towns are seen from the summit of the hill; in a lovely valley the frontier line; looking towards France you get a view of the Spicheren Berg, the scene of the memorable engagement; on both sides large forests stretch as far as the vision reaches. Forbach is concealed by the opposite hills, or mountains as they are more properly called; but Styringen and its tall factory chimneys are plainly visible.

It was in the valley and on the slopes of the hill at Bellevue that the outposts, of both armies were stationed; and it was here that officers, correspondents, and peasants used to assemble daily in expectation of witnessing the commencement of hostilities in earnest. Here it was that we awaited the attack. The scene on those early days of the campaign was remarkable. "Not a drum was heard," nor the sound of a *chassepôt* or, *zünt-nadel*, save on rare occasions. The foreposts contented themselves with watching each other's movements. Now and then, when some of the more adventurous German *vorposten* approached too near to the line of demarcation, we heard the sharp whizz of a bullet, a compliment usually returned from the Prussian side, and then all was silent for several hours.

From the brow of the hill at Bellevue we could see the Fransozen *vedettes*, and a few tents: that was all. The most persistent visitor to Bellevue was Captain Seaton, of the British army, who thought it no waste of time to remain all the morning on the lookout from an advanced position. This gentleman, seated on his camp-stool, offered an excellent target for the enemy, had they chosen to take advantage of his daring. He had, I believe, one or two narrow escapes while engaged in making a reconnaissance with a small body of Prussian soldiers; but he was not deterred from continuing his observations by the whistle of a bullet or the proximity of a French cavalryman.

It was necessary to have special military permission to visit Bellevue. Two of my Press friends who had failed to secure an authorization suffered for their neglect of this precaution by being arrested as spies, and marched between a file of men to the officer in command, who at once released them upon receiving their assurance that they were English journalists. It will perhaps be remembered that it was in this locality that the French fired several shots even before war had been formally declared; and it was here that the following incident occurred on the 29th of July. Some peasants who had visited the hill out of curiosity, waited there for several hours in the hope of witnessing an advance by the French. Suddenly there was a report, a sharp whistle in the air, a loud explosion, and an equally loud exclamation from the landlord of the little tavern on the hill, caused by the bursting of a grenade in the "bar."

A second grenade followed the first, breaking the windows of the inn, scattering fragments of glass amongst the occupants of the room in which the missiles fell, but hurting nobody, although the tavern-keeper was standing at his counter when the explosions took place. In one corner of the apartment hung a cage containing a bird. A piece of grenade struck the cage, destroyed the door, and gave liberty to the little songster, which, it may be, was a starling, pining like Sterne's bird, and chanting all day—"I can't get out! I can't get out!"

Confronting one another in this manner, the foreposts of both armies stood for several days, and I need not dwell upon the monotony of the time. The hotels at Saarbrucken and St. Johann were full of officers and correspondents. The gentlemen of the Press mustered largely. Every hotel had a special reporter amongst its guests, the Rheinischer Hof and the Hotel Hagen being the houses principally patronized. We had newspaper representatives from all quarters—from London, Dublin, Glasgow, Manchester, Vienna, Berlin, Cologne, Now York, and Frankfort-on-the-Maine; and although of news there was usually *rien*, everybody felt constrained to send off a daily letter to his journal. Over these communications much midnight oil was burnt, for no one cared to write by daylight.

After the matutinal walk to Bellevue our time—I speak for four or five gentlemen and myself—was usually occupied in visiting those persons who had horses to dispose of, and in trying those animals which looked worth anything. The trials usually ended in a long consultation as to the merits of the steeds, and an offer to give about half the price demanded by their owners, who were as difficult to deal with as the horse-dealers at an English country fair. At first we were resolved upon going to the war—when it began—with as much state as possible; and it was facetiously suggested by a Vienna gentleman that a roomy vehicle should be purchased and called "the Correspondents' carriage." But the proposed arrangement fell through owing to various circumstances, over some of which we certainly had no control, and the end of it was that everybody resolved upon shifting for himself.

There was a general desire to assume a military appearance, to which end revolvers and high boots were purchased; and not even the renowned Mr. Jos. Sedley, as Mr. Thackeray depicted that worthy before the Battle of Waterloo, looked more formidable than our party of Press-men. The editors of the *Morning Advertiser*, the *Manchester Guardian*, the *Vienna Old Press*, the *Vienna*

New Press, and various other journals would have been more than satisfied could they have seen their "Specials" equipped for the campaign at Saarbrucken. But a busier time was fast approaching for those to whom was entrusted the onerous duty of chronicling the incidents of the campaign. An unimportant affair between the foreposts preceded the engagement at Saarbrucken on the 2nd of August. The only damage done on the former occasion was the partial destruction of the tavern at Bellevue to which I have briefly referred.

On the evening of the 1st of August, our little Press detachment turned out to see a Prussian battalion, in bivouac, about a mile and a half from St. Johann, the party including Mr. Archibald Forbes,[1] who has done such good service for the *Daily News* by his admirable descriptions and exceeding energy. On the following morning I left my hotel and paid a second visit to the bivouac. The battalion encamped here had no reason to apprehend an attack, and the men were dispersed about the neighbouring fields and orchards. I had walked through the encampment, and was seeking some shelter from the heat, when a mounted orderly, covered with dust, galloped up and delivered an order, the affect which was magical.

The bivouac was broken up, the artillery was limbered up, and the whole battalion was under arms in about a quarter of an hour. It was no time for delay, for the news brought by the orderly was that the enemy had driven in the Prussian *vorposten* at Bellevue, and had taken up position on the heights commanding Saarbruck. Looking towards the heights, I saw formidable array of French soldiers, and artillery planted behind entrenchments which had been thrown up with great rapidity. Several Prussian detachments were soon marching across the fields towards the railway bridge near Barbach; almost simultaneously with this movement some grenades and bullets flew over our heads; and all was bustle and animation. *The war had begun!*

---

1. *Britain in Afghanistan 1: the First Afghan War 1839-42*, and, *Britain in Afghanistan 2: the Second Afghan War 1878-80* by Archibald Forbes also published by Leonaur.

CHAPTER 5

Under Fire for the First Time

My position at this moment was not a pleasant one. Having been unable at that time to procure a "Legitimation," which indeed none of the Press fraternity then possessed, I was in danger of being arrested as a spy when hostilities commenced, or at least of being sent to the rear with considerable haste. Immediately the French, who occupied the heights of Saarbrucken under General Frosssard, began to open fire, I followed a detachment of infantry through the fields, towards the ruined bridge across the Saar at Barbach, making notes of the relative position of the two armies as I went along. For a few minutes I was permitted to pursue my vocation and my walk uninterruptedly; but I had not gone far when a Prussian officer rode up to me, and asked what I was doing. Something like the following ensued.

Officer. "What are you doing here, sir?"
Myself. "Reporting the movements of the troops."
Officer. "Who are you, then?"
Myself. "I am the Correspondent of the ———."
Officer. "Have you a '*legitimation*'?"
Myself. "No."
Officer. "Then I am afraid we cannot allow you to remain here."
Myself. "But it is necessary for me to be here."
Officer. "We don't know if you are what you represent yourself to be, or a Fransozen spy!"
Myself. "I am an English Correspondent, and I request per-

mission to be allowed to perform my duties. I am acquainted with Lieutenant ——— of the *landwehr*, who was here in bivouac this morning; he will satisfy you that I am what I profess to be."

Officer. "Very well. In that case you may remain here."

I was going towards Barbach, where the French infantry had appeared, when I heard a terrific cannonade to my left, and nearer to the town of Saarbrucken. I therefore returned to the *plateau* upon which the Prussian cannon were ranged, and found myself all at once in the thick of the fire. The *chaussée* runs close by this point, and here grenades and *chassepôt* bullets were falling by the thousand. The trees which line the roadway were falling everywhere, their branches were cut off by the grenades, and it was impossible to find what would have been regarded as a tolerably safe place. It was the first time I had been under fire, and I confess the sensation was more novel than agreeable.

The sound of a grenade or a *chassepôt*, heard for the first time, has a singular effect upon the mind. You don't know whether to advance, or stand still, or run away; and at every report you believe the deadly missile is coming straight at you. This creates a desire to dodge every shrapnel and bullet that comes forward, sometimes accompanied by an insane desire to put yourself into the smallest possible compass, or to get behind something that offers the slightest protection, if it is only a bean stick. From the heights opposite the *plateau*, on which the Prussian position had been made, came a continuous blaze of light.

All along the hill-top the French had placed their artillery (four and eight pounders), to protect which they had thrown up entrenchments during the night. From this point they poured a raking fire upon the Prussians, who had nothing in the shape of earthworks to shield them. Indeed, as far as we were concerned, it was a fight in the open. For an hour the batteries of the Germans kept their position but shortly after 12 o'clock I heard the order given to retire, and in a few minutes the Prussians were in full retreat. I scrambled over *débris* of trees &c., into the road, and prepared for a run; on all sides of me were Prussian soldiers retreating in tolerably good order. The artillery flew past me, closely followed by the infantry, and followed also by grenades, and shrapnel, and bullets; for the French, directly they saw us in retreat, recommenced their fire, which they had been suffered to languish a little.

There are immense forests in the neighbourhood of the action, and through these went the *soldaten* pell-mell. The road was full of soldiers, horses, and peasants, the latter with blanched cheeks and trembling limbs, begging the Prussians to "give them a lift." One old woman, who had a child with her, succeeded in persuading a soldier to allow her to ride on a baggage waggon; but there was no room for the little one, who would have been left behind and trampled to death, but for the kindness of an artilleryman, who took the girl in his arms, and was rewarded by "*merci bien, mon brave*," a thousand times repeated.

To be out of the way of the gun-carriages which were galloping by every moment, I threaded my steps through the intricacies of a path skirting the forest, keeping up with the soldiers as well as I could. It was impossible, however, to make much way, for the path was interlaced with brambles and branches, and every other minute the unpleasant whistle and startling "*boom!*" of a grenade, falling in front or close behind me, made it necessary to "dodge" the missiles and make frequent *détours*, In the forest glades the peasants—men, women, and children—were vainly attempting to find shelter from the enemy's fire, which increased rather than slackened.

The day was one of the hottest conceivable, and after a run of between one and two hours I was obliged to throw myself down under a giant oak tree, by the side of the road, where I watched the soldiers gallop by, and listened to the cannonade of the enemy in the distance. Beneath the grateful shade afforded by the spreading branches of this monarch of the forest I penned the account of my first engagement—my desk being the leaf-covered ground, and my chair the gnarled roots of a tree. When I had finished my description of the battle, I hastened along the road in the rear of the defeated Prussians, expecting every moment to be overtaken by the enemy's cavalry, or even by a regiment of infantry. It turned out, however, that we were not pursued; and I reached without hindrance a small wayside inn.

The road in front of the tavern was crowded by soldiers. The wounded were being taken into the inn, and I shall never forget the horror of the villagers as each blood-covered man was brought forward. The women and girls wept over the mangled bodies, and the children ran crying into the houses. In the road there was as much mirth as though instead of a defeat it had been a victory. The *soldaten*, seated under the trees by the side of the road, or astride a heap of felled timber, quaffed their red wine, ate their bread and *speck*, and smoked as unconcernedly as though the enemy were no nearer than Paris, instead of within an hour's march.

Late in the afternoon I left the Prussians, and returned towards St. Johann, having previously refreshed myself by a two hours' nap in the forest, from which I was awakened by some soldiers, whose impression that I was a Fransozen I soon removed by wishing them *"guten abend,"* and giving them some cigars. When I arrived at the scene of the battle, what a change had come over the landscape! The road was strewn with branches of trees, bits of grenade and shrapnel, rifle bullets, pieces of uniform, a *züntnadel* or two, a sword-bayonet here and there. What had been verdant fields in the morning were now charred wastes.

A little inn near the bivouac was in flames; along the road were dead and mangled horses; near St. Johann I found other cottages burnt down; and when I reached the town I found the Hotel Hagen deserted, the bedroom next to mine utterly destroyed by the French bombardment, the houses battered by the grenades, and the front of the railway station half destroyed. Very few people were in the streets. The French had not occupied the town, though they had entered Saarbrucken, and remained a short time. I looked out from my room at the hotel upon the heights beyond the Saar, where, without the help of my glass, I could see the French in large numbers walking backwards and forwards, and occasionally throwing a grenade or discharging a *chassepôt*.

There was not a Prussian soldier to be seen—all had retreated; my friends of the Press had gone I knew not whither: and I had the pleasure of finding myself alone in the bombarded town of St. Johann, with the French cannons on the neighbouring heights, and a probability that at nightfall the cannonade would be resumed, and the defenceless town destroyed

Chapter 6

In Search of a Legitimation

The expectation of a second bombardment was not at all conducive to sleep; so, with the French cannon pointing grimly at the town, and the red glare of the camp-fires plainly visible from my bedroom, I sat up all night, writing and wondering what would come next. No shots were fired that night, and the following morning I walked up to the railway station to post my letters to London, I might as well have endeavoured to send my correspondence to the Styx! The station and post-office officials had fled on the previous day immediately the bombardment began; and there was not a soul on the platform who could give me any information One side of the station exhibited unmistakable evidences of the bombardment.

There were great holes in the walls, every window was shattered, the large refreshment-room was a heap of ruins, and a workshop on the other side of the *bahn* was so damaged that all the workmen had deserted it. There were no trains, and it was impossible to send telegrams or letters. A placard, hastily affixed to the booking-office window, informed those of the public who were interested in the announcement that all business and traffic would be suspended until further notice! To a newspaper correspondent with his battle reports ready for dispatch this was "a heavy blow and sore discouragement."

But there was no help for it; and I returned to the hotel, strapped on my knapsack, and without further delay left St. Johann in the hope of over taking the soldiers of the Eighth Prussian Army Corps, with whom I had been on the previous day, and in anxious expectation of securing such a *Legitimation* as would enable me to move about freely and without being subjected to arrest. The *haupt-quartier* of General von Göben was at Lebach, a small town in the Rhine provinces. My way from Saarbrucken was over the same ground I had traversed the day before, and I had to pass across the fields which were the scene of the first battle.

It was not by any means an agreeable walk. Three divisions of French troops with twenty-three cannon still occupied the heights of the drill-ground, and amused themselves by firing upon everybody they saw. I did not meet a single pedestrian—not a Prussian soldier was to be seen. The trees by the side of the *chaussée* afforded little protection from *chassepôt* bullets, several of which flew past me as I walked across the blackened *plateau*. The houses which the grenades had set in flames were by this time either quite razed to the ground or still smouldering, and the villagers stood looking on at the ruin with sad hearts. Two miles from St. Johann I came upon the Prussian *vorposten*, by whom I was not challenged save by a cheery "*Guten Tag, mein Herr.*"

I passed along the road over which the defeated Germans had marched, and through the forest, occasionally meeting or overtaking the German inhabitants, or a soldier. I had walked perhaps eight miles on my way to Lebach, when, observing some more *vorposten*, I asked them the distance to that town. They replied by inquiring who I was, what I wanted at Lebach, and where I came from. I answered these questions, and, with an instinctive sense of danger, bade them "*Guten Morgen.*" But I was not to escape in this manner. "*Nein, nein!*" they shouted in my ears, and surrounding me, asked, "*Was wollen sie hier macken.*'

"*Ich bin Correspondenten von Englishen Zeitung,*" was my answer, given in as angry a tone as that which they had adopted towards me; and I made another attempt to move off.

"*Nein, nein,*" the corporal cried, "*Komt sie mit!*"

I was surrounded by a dozen fierce-looking Prussians, who would doubtless have been only too glad had I endeavoured to escape and given them the opportunity to shoot me down as a Fransozen spy. It was of no use to remonstrate, so I walked on through the stubble in silence, smoking my cigar with as much unconcern as I could assume under peculiarly disagreeable circumstances. Two miles walk across the fields, and we arrived at a bivouac. My captors announced to the captain the circumstances under which I was arrested, and painted my case in the blackest possible colours, insisting that as I had come from Saarbrucken I must be a spy.

"*Wo komt sie?*" asked the captain.
"*Saarbrucken.*"
"*Wo gehen sie?*"
"*Nach Lebach, zu der General von Göben.*"
"*Haben sie eine legitimation?*"
"*Nein, mein Herr. Ich wünschen eine legitimation.*"

This concluded our dialogue. Some orders wrere given to two of the soldiers who had arrested me, and I was ordered to accompany them to the *Oberst*. This gentleman was asleep at his quarters, and did not appear at all pleased at being awakened. I told him who and what I was, and what I wanted, and he instructed my escort to hand me over to some hussars who were in bivouac a mile or two farther on. I was very kindly received by some officers here, and informed by them that two English officers were in the neighbourhood. This was gratifying news, and would have been the more so had my informant had the least notion of the whereabouts of my countrymen, who were not to be found.

I was told that I should be taken to Lebach, where, upon satisfying General von Göben that I was what I represented myself be, I should doubtless receive a *legitimation*. Under the escort of a hussar I again marched on, beneath the fierce rays of the August sun—with nothing to eat or drink, and no hope obtaining any. My escort, who rode by my side with his faded carbine in his hand, vouchsafed me no other remark but "*vorwarts!*" which he shouted whenever I asked permission to rest. We passed several thousand Prussian troops; indeed, half of the whole German forces were massed in this neighbourhood, although that fact was not known at Saarbrucken. That the Prussians at this time were not prepared for an attack, I am sure, and equally confident that had the French followed up their easy victory on the 2nd of August, they would have probably changed the whole course of events.

After marching in silence for a couple of hours, causing the greatest delight to the *soldaten*, who ran down to the road by thousands directly they saw me, I met the Oberst von Witzendorff, chief of the General Staff of the Eighth Army Corps. To him I explained my case, and requested to be released; but I was informed that only General von Göben could give such an order. Colonel von Witzendorff promised to speak to the general on my behalf, and said in the meantime I must make myself as comfortable as possible at the hotel at Lebach. Along the dusty road again we marched—my throat parched with thirst, and the fatigue occasioned by the long walk increasing every moment. We passed through several villages, full of soldiers, ere we came to Lebach, and I had some difficulty in escaping ill-treatment— the brutal hussar who escorted me leading his comrades to believe that I was a French spy.

I found Lebach crowded with troops. The moment we arrived in front of the hotel where the *haupt-quartier* was temporarily fixed, the officers flocked to the windows, and the soldiers surrounded me. My escort having to leave me to enter the hotel, gave me in charge of a soldier, who at once laid his hand upon my shoulder to prevent my escape—a piece of audacity which I rewarded by raising my stick and cutting the brute across the shoulder with it. I never saw a man look more astonished. He was wild with rage, and was proceeding to slang me when there was a movement in the crowd, and looking round, I saw a tall *cuirassier* officer coming to my rescue, and lashing right and left with his cane. This gentleman invited me into the hotel, and prevented me from being forcibly put in the common guard-room.

By the same friendly officer I was taken into the apartment

occupied by him and his brother-officers, who received me with the greatest kindness, I dined with them, and passed the remainder of the eventful day pleasantly enough in their agreeable society and in that of a gentleman who represented, as special artist, a Leipzig illustrated *zeitung*. The house was full of officers and soldiers, and when the hour for retiring came I looked around for a bed. I might as well have expected to find all the comforts of a West-End hotel. There was not an unoccupied bed in the house—not even a couch or an armchair.

I went into every room, but they were crowded by soldiers, sleeping altogether on the floor, and there was not sufficient space for the smallest drummer-boy in the service. The landlord did not appear inclined to accede to my request for some straw on which to sleep in the dining-room; but upon being interrogated by a lieutenant of *cuirassiers*, he brought in a large heap of straw, upon which, with every bone aching, I threw myself, but not to sleep. I was not the only occupant of the apartment. Three or four *sous-officièrs* were sleeping near me; and about midnight, hearing voices in the room, I looked up and saw General von Göben and some of his staff poring over maps and discussing a projected attack. I think I shall not be far wrong when I say that the general of the Eighth Army Corps was planning his movements for the following Thursday and Saturday, the 4th and 6th of August, on which days were fought the great Battles of Wörth, Weissemburg, and Saarbrucken.

The next morning found me still a prisoner, unable to leave the *haupt-quartier*. I saw General von Göben, but, although the particulars of my arrest had been laid before him, and although the Oberst von Witzendorff had said to me, "I quite believe all that you have said—I am sure you are no spy," despite these circumstances, I was informed that I must go to Trier and have an interview with General von Steinmetz, the commander of the First German Army. Accordingly at eight o'clock I was conducted to a *voiture*, the driver of which made me as comfortable as he could by spreading straw upon the rough boards, and, with a hussar at each side of the wagon, we followed in the wake of the Eighth Army Corps.

Our way was through the Rhine provinces— through a wonderfully fertile agricultural country, diversified by magnificent forests and smiling valleys. Between Lebach and Trier I think I must have seen half a million of troops, who were being massed here, and marching to various points on the frontier. There was the same curiosity to see "the spy" as had been displayed on the previous day, and my carriage was frequently surrounded by burly soldiers, some of whom, compassionating my condition, offered me *schnaps*, beer, and cigars. From Lebach to Trier was a journey of five hours, over abominable roads; but I cheerfully submitted to the little *désagrémens* of the ride in the full assurance that directly I reached Trier, General Steinmetz would order me to be released.

Alas for the fatuity of human hopes! The general was not at Trier, and we had perforce to await his coming. The soldiers who formed my escort were quartered in the town, and I was obliged to go with them in the search for their quarters. These were in a poor cottage tenanted by a wretchedly-clad woman and two children, who were all lamenting the death of the humble bread-winner of the house. I was conducted into a garret, the only furniture in which were a couple of chairs, a straw mattress, and a rude table, and here the *soldaten* brought me a flask of wine and a little bread.

In the town we found a *restauration*, where I had the pleasure of entertaining my custodians, who, hearing that General Steinmetz had come into Trier, hurried me to the general's quarters. My letter of introduction from General von Göben was not, it appeared, of a very satisfactory nature, for, after scowling at me, his Excellency asked me for my passport and papers. I frankly stated that these documents were at Saarbruken, and that I was in search of a "*legitimation.*"

"*Wo gehen sie?*" growled his Excellency.

"*Ich bin Correspondenten von Englischen Zeitung und wünschen gern in das haupt-quartier zu gelassen werden,*" I answered, respectfully. I added inadvertently, "*Vous parlez Français, probablement, M.

le Général?"

This sealed my fate. "*Parlez Frangais!*" he shouted. "*Sprecher sie Deutsch?*" And, his face red with anger, his Excellency, with surpassing politeness, tore up my card before me, and threw the pieces of innocent pasteboard on the ground. General Steinmetz was the only Prussian officer I met who did not speak French.

I was relegated back to General von Göben, whose headquarters had that day been changed from Lebach to Ottweiler. I suppose the Prussians thought they had conveyed me far enough without demanding any remuneration, for I was told that I must hire a carriage to take me to Ottweiler, about twenty miles from Trier.

The "carriage" was a waggon of the kind happily only seen in Germany and France. A villainous-looking young fellow demanded nine *thalers* (£1.7s.) or this vehicle, and I had the benefit of another twenty miles' ride over newly-made roads, the charioteer urging on his horses at a speed worthy of Jehu, the son of Nimshi.

When we reached the *haupt-quartier* at Ottweiler I was so stiff from this unusual mode of conveyance that I could hardly walk. Upon alighting at the door of the hotel, I was honoured with the usual *levée*, "the Fransozen spy" attracting general attention. I entered the audience-room, and found myself again in the company of my friends of the general staff, who were amused and surprised at my presence. I had to stand a good deal of "chaff," and then a consultation took place between General von Göben and the heads of the staff. It was evident they were embarrassed as to what should be done with me. I was far more difficult to deal with than a genuine Fransozen *espion*, for there was a doubt as to my real position,

I had been arrested, however, and military custom demanded my detention until the mystery which enveloped me was cleared up. Ultimately, I received from General von Göben a document ordering me to go to Cologne for my papers, and I was released from custody. Although I was only a prisoner for two days, I can well imagine the extravagant feelings of delight which fill the mind of Mr. Sykes when he "comes out" after a twelvemonths' incarceration for burglary. My sensations upon finding myself at liberty again were of the liveliest, and I walked through the little streets of Ottweiler as gleefully as though I were pacing the flags of Pall Mall, It is all very well for the poet to sing—

Stone walls do not a prison make,
Nor iron bars a cage.

I should like the poet to be under military arrest for forty-eight hours in an enemy's country where every suspect was liable to be shot at ten minutes' notice. Under those circumstances, the poet would sing a different song, you may depend upon it,

I left for Cologne the same night, slept at St. Wendel, the nest station to Ottweiler, and went on the next morning to Bingerbruck. It is a four hours' ride in peace-times; but on this occasion we were thirteen hours and a half in train. Bingerbruck is a large junction station with lines to Mainz and Darmstadt, Saarbrucken, Wiesbaden, Coblentz, Cologne, and many other places—not unlike Bishopstoke, on the South-Western Railway, I ascertained that a train was going to Cologne at 8 a.m., and decided to leave at that hour. The difficulty was, however, to know from which platform the train would start.

It is a wilderness of a place, Bingerbruck station on a dark, wet night—a single light casting its uncertain glimmer on the platform, and the refreshment-room full of officers waiting for their trains. Two or three officials, who had taken more *schnaps* than they ought to have drank, were the only persons who could have given me any information respecting the train for Cologne. They were, however, so thick in speech, and so generally bemused with drinking of strong waters, that I could get nothing out of them.

In this strait I mooned about the railway until I found a soldier-train, which I ascertained was certainly going to Coblentz, and probably to Cologne. It was a luggage train; full of baggage and soldiers; and it went at the extraordinary speed of about three miles an hour. I reached Cologne late in the afternoon, and found the town of Jean Maria Farina in the greatest excitement, owing to the rumours of a great victory by the German troops, who had, indeed, fought and routed the French at Weissemburg.

Chapter 7

At Cologne Again

It was my good fortune to be in Cologne on the Sunday following the great Prussian victories at Weissemburg, Wörth, and Saarbrucken, The news of the Saturday's battles arrived on Sunday morning, and immediately the whole city notified of the intelligence. The bells rang, flags were hung out, bands paraded, the streets were crowded with people, the *cafés* were full, the newspaper offices were thronged, and everybody was reading the *affiches* on the walls, I never saw a people so quickly infected with delirious excitement. In the *cafés* they were singing "*Die Wacht am Rhein!*" and making fun of "the *Mitrailleuse Prinz*," as they christened the Prince Imperial, who it was reported had fired the first *mitrailleuse* at Saarbrucken on the previous Tuesday. The scenes at the *restaurations* were both amusing and exciting.

You saw an obese German with his arms round the neck of a lank youth, who vainly struggled to free himself from the unwelcome embrace; students were there, brimful of patriotism, chanting *Kriegs-lied* one after the other; glasses were clinked to the honour of Germany, and glasses were also broken in honour of the Fatherland; there was no end to the enthusiasm. A word *en parenthèse anent* "*Die Wacht am Rhein*," It was written in 1840 by Max Schneckenburger, who was born at Thalheim, Wurtemberg. The words were set to music by several composers (Erck and Greef, according to a writer in the *Athenaeum*, first set it in the "*Chorliedersammlung für Schulem*"), but the only tune that now lives is that composed by Carl Wilhelm, a poor schoolmaster of Thuringen.

Until the war broke out Herr Wilhelm was unknown save to a small circle of acquaintance; but when there was talk of the French marching to the Rhine, somebody remembered Carl's song; it was dragged out of its obscurity, and all through Germany nothing was heard but the stirring strains of "*Die Wacht am Rhein!*"

The melody, I find, has become well-known in England. Perhaps, therefore, it will not be considered out of place if I introduce the following translation of the famous song, in which I have endeavoured to preserve, as much as possible, the rough, warlike character of Schneckenburger's words:—

Die Wacht am Rhein.

1

It blows a call like thunder,
Like waves that rise and fall:
To the stream! To the Rhine! The German Rhine
We hear the trumpet call!
Dear Fatherland! Dear Fatherland!
O rest thee, country mine,
Solid and true, in armour clad,
Is the watch of the German Rhine!
Dear Fatherland! Dear Fatherland!
O rest thee, country mine,
Solid and true, in armour clad,
Is the watch of the German Rhine!

2

The watchword, "God and Fatherland,"
Is flash'd from East to West;
Men's eyes are sparkling brightly,
And courage fills each breast.
Earnest and strong we muster,
On the brink we take our stand,
To save from the ruthless foemen
The stream of the Holy Land.

3
We look aloft to Heaven,
To the fields of Paradise—
There our fathers look down with love
As they see their children rise,
And swear with patriot ardour,
"We'll know no peace or rest
Till the Rhine, the Rhine of the Fatherland,
Is free as a German's breast!"

4
Whilst a drop of blood is left us,
Whilst our hand a sword can wield,
Whilst we've strength to load a rifle
To none will Germans yield!
Our watch-cry, then, is "Fatherland!"
Let none stand idly by—
To the Rhine! The Rhine—the German Rhine!
Its loving guardians fly!

In the evening of this exciting day I witnessed an illumination of Cologne. By nine o'clock the old city was a blaze of red and white lights. It was like a scene from the *Arabian Nights*—a night *fête* of unparalleled splendour in the annals of Cologne. And it was all done by candles! The large establishment of the Farinas in the Dom Kloster was splendidly illuminated and formed a wonderful contrast to the Dom, which stood grandly out, lit up as it was, a mass of architecture of marvellous proportions and rare beauty. All the hotels were illuminated with much taste. The streets were almost impassable from the number of carriages full of ladies and children, in summer *toilettes*; bands of soldiers and young men paraded the town, singing with great unction a humorous song, wedded to a lively air of Offenbach's, detailing how that at length they had "stopped the mouth of Napoleon," the chorus being a repetition of the last syllable in the word "*chassepôt*."

All the way down the Komodien Strasse were Chinese lanterns, rows of candles on the window-sills, and occasionally gas jets. Drooping in the still air of a sultry summer night—black cloud-masses forming a back-ground of great grandeur—were the black and white, and black and yellow, white and red, and pure white flags of the various German nationalities; and between all this display of bunting glimmered the lights. The candles threw a mellow glare upon flags, and people, and streets, giving to the mass of colour that warm tint which you may see in the paintings of the Dutch school. Illuminated for the German victories, the Komodien Strasse looked like a bit taken from a picture by Teniers or Quentin Matsys. The Hohe Strasse was the same.

By an excellent arrangement of the police, there was not much difficulty in getting by way of the Hohe Strasse into the Haymarket (which, by the way, is not at all like our London thoroughfare), and so into the Old Market—a broad *Platz*, surrounded by trees, and in the rear of the Rath Haus, a glorious specimen of thirteenth-century Gothic architecture, with gables and buttresses, and mullioned windows. Coloured lanterns were hung in the trees; and as we were waiting for the expected appearance of the torch-bearers, a murmur of admiration came from the crowd, and looking up into the black sky, we saw that the heavens were made less sombre by the ruddy glare of the red fire which was at that moment lit on the tower of the Rath Haus.

Nothing more picturesque can be conceived. From the tower depended flags, upon which the dull red glare fell as they fluttered in the lighteat of winds; every pinnacle and window, and the cross surmounting the building, stood out with marvellous distinctness; the tower was bathed in a wealth of crimson colour. I turned round to apologize for standing in the way of a pretty *fraulein*, whose *piqué* dress and scarlet bow came out well in that flood of light, and when I looked up again at the Rath Haus Tower the lights had disappeared, and everybody was murmuring applausively and averring that the sight had been *wunterschön*.

CHAPTER 8

After the Battle

After the battle! As I write the words, how many painful reminiscences are evoked! They call to mind the glorious sight of battalions marching at dawn of day through, quiet country places—marching gaily to give battle to the enemy; marching with full confidence in their strength, and in full reliance upon their leaders. The bands play, the soldiers sing, the bayonets and swords glisten in the summer sun, the horses champ their hits, and the scared peasants run to their doors to see the brave show. Six days ago I watched whole army corps marching or riding to Weissemburg, to Wörth, Saarbrucken; today many of the same men pass and repass me on the platform of Cologne railway station.

The same men? Can these maimed and wounded *soldaten* be of those whom I saw but yesterday, as it were, in all the plenitude of their splendid strength? Yester-night we celebrated the three great victories; today we sorrowfully receive and tend the wounded! If you remember the numbers of the killed and of those put temporarily *hors de combat* in the three battles, Weissemburg. Wörth, and Saarbrucken, you will be the better able to appreciate the scenes I am about to describe. At Weissemburg the losses of the French and Prussians were each between 5,000 and 6,000 killed and wounded—the latter being generally left in the hands of the victors.

At Saarbruck the total Prussian loss was 5,000 single division losing 1,800 killed and wounded in the gallant storming of the heights of Spicheren and Forbach. At Wörth their loss was about the same. Take the Prussian dead and wounded only, in those three battles, and you get a total of 15,000, which is rather under than over the mark. Subtract a third of that number as being dead, and that leaves 10,000 Prussians wounded in three days—a trifle when compared with the 28,000 Frenchmen killed and wounded between Metz and Nancy later in August, and the bloody affair near Gorze on the 16th, 17th, and 18th of the same month, when the Prussian loss in killed and wounded was 48,000, and that of the French 51,000!

The platform of the railway station at Cologne, then, this present 9th of August, presents a very woeful spectacle—such an one as the war artist usually manages to beep in the background of his pictures. The platform, the approaches to the station, the waiting-rooms, the offices—all are full of wounded soldiers. There is hardly a man wearing an uniform who has not some hurt. Here is a private of the 48th—the regiment which suffered more severely than any other, in the engagement at Saarbrucken, on the 6th of August: his head is bound up with linen, but the bandage does not conceal his gaping wounds.

There you see an artilleryman in a torn and jagged uniform—limping about with one foot in a slipper, one arm in a sling, his wan face unshaven, and unwashed, and bloody. On yonder bench, next to a wounded hussar, is another 48th man, lying prone on his back, unable to move, and calling, with what voice he may, for ice to cool the fever which is raging within him. Here it another, wounded in both legs, which dangle helplessly, and you may see the salt tears course down his bronzed, whiskered face, strive howsoever he may to stop them. And in truth, "the unaccustomed brine" is in the eyes of many a witness of this direful scene.

Look at yonder window, where stand the German maidens and matrons, and mark their red and swollen eyes. See these comely market women survey with sorrow the stricken men who crowd the platform, and stand around the doorways, and lie about in the large room devoted to hospital purposes; watch them, I say, and then tell me if you can look unmoved and tearless upon these mangled heroes. I have said "stricken *men*;" but there be many here who have not yet entered on manhood—mere boys, whom it was cruel to drag from their homes. I have in my mind's eye one lad who, I dare affirm, had bound his lacerated and bleeding hand in the very handkerchief his sweetheart gave him the night before he joined his company—a blur silk handkerchief, with white spots; if you could have examined it you might have found in one corner, carefully worked, the words—"*Hans. Von Gretchen.*"

Lying about on this Cologne platform, and in the *Lazareth*, these heroes of Weissemburg, and Wörth, and Saarbrucken, are objects, of compassion to everyone. Not a soul amongst the spectators but is anxious to assist the *verwunden*; for these lazy, unambitious, despised Germans plead guilty to the grave charge of loving one another. Amateur nurses—concerning whom further mention is subsequently made—abounded; and the patriotism of the German ladies who engaged in this work cannot be too highly extolled. The wounded were supplied with *butterbrod, schinken, kase,* wine, beer, coffee, and excellent soup.

During at least the early part of the war time Cologne metaphorically overflowed with milk and honey. Many of the wounded I had seen at Saarbrucken in bivouac, or on the day of the French attack, or, with some, I had retreated to Reiselburg. There were the men of the 39th, 48th, and 60th regiments, artillery as well as infantry. Poor fellows! when I saw them on the frontier they were full of eager anxiety to be led onwards. Since then they had faced the leaden hail which fell in front of and around them, and here was the result—skulls laid bare, legs shot off, hands and arms crushed, and frames enfeebled from loss of blood.

"It is the fortune of war, *mein Herr*," said one of these maimed warriors to me; "it is my turn today, and it may be yours tomorrow." As the long trains left the station for the provinces, the wounded soldiers, whose courage never deserted them, sang "*Ich bin ein Preussen,*" or "*Die Wacht am Rhein!*" Those on the platform seemed at first disposed to take up the chorus of Herr Wilhelm's song; but we were in no mood for singing, and turned sorrowfully away as the last carriage disappeared.

CHAPTER 9

En Route to the Front

On the 10th of August I again left Cologne, bound for "the front"—a position to which every correspondent was ordered by his editor, who little knew the perils which beset the war journalists. I took a ticket to Bingerbruck, which was as far as you could be booked at Cologne. There were very few soldiers in our train on this occasion, but many men journeying to the front to assist the German wounded. I met a young Englishman who had come from the south of France for his sister, who was at a school on the Rhine, where she and her friends were left by the proprietress, who had fled to Belgium directly the war broke out.

Arrived at Bingerbruck, I found that the regular traffic was stopped, and that only military trains were running. As I was inquiring at the booking-office how and when I could get on, assistance was volunteered me by one of the most dilapidated gentlemen it has ever been my lot to meet. He was one of the amateur *sanitaats*-men, as the red cross on his arm testified. He had drank so much cognac *en voyage* that his utterance was unpleasantly thick, and at times incomprehensible. His offer to act as pilot to me was embarrassing, for his extraordinary mode of speech and general raggedness attracted universal attention. However, be had an official permission to rove about where he pleased, and I put myself under his guidance, the more particularly as he stated that he was going to Saarbrucken, I soon found two places in a train full of soldiers—a portion of the Eighth

Army Corps; and after laying in a store of provisions—*butterbrod* and wine—I made myself as comfortable in a horse box as circumstances permitted.

Our carriage contained four horses and seven or eight men, besides my good-natured friend and myself. "We left Bingerbruck about two o'clock, and had hopes of reaching Saarbrucken the same night. We passed through the charming valley of the Nahe at a funereal pace, which argued ill for an early termination of the journey. At every station the people ran down to meet the train and to distribute provisions and cigars to the soldiers, many of whom had never been so feasted before. Sunset saw us shunted on a siding near Oberstein, where we remained all night, performing our ablutions on the following morning in small puddles of dirty water by the roadside, using our pocket handkerchiefs as towels.

About noon we moved on slowly, but pulled up again in the course a three or four hours, and passed another night in the train, the endless discomforts of which I need not allude to, because everybody can imagine what they were. At four o'clock the next morning I arose, jaded and stiff, from attempting to the floor of the carriage. There was brick-yard close to where the long train was standing, and here we found sufficient water in a tub to wash with. From the villagers we purchased a little bread and cheese and wine, and lighting the inevitable pipe, waited until the order came for the train to move on to Saarbruck, from which we were distant only about four miles.

Eight hours were thus occupied, at the expiration of which, all in our carriage—soldiers as well as civilians—unable to bear this eternal delay, left the train and set out for St. Johann, where we arrived hungry, dirty, and generally "done-up," just in time for dinner. The first person I met at St. Johann was the correspondent of a Vienna journal; it was this gentleman who had inadvertently announced my death in his paper and he welcomed me as one who had risen from the grave. I found the Rheinischer Hof full of officers and newspaper correspondents, and it was only after much persuasion that I got a bed there.

At dinner at the *table d'hôte* of the Rheinischer Hof between thirty and forty gentlemen usually sat down, the majority being officers, expecting to go forward every day. The senior officer was placed at the head of the table; we civilians were interspersed among the *militaires*; and the mid-day meal (for the Germans dine at one o'clock) passed pleasantly enough. Nothing was talked of but the war, which engrossed our undivided attention. Regiments marched daily, with bands playing, but with their colours furled and cased. These, it must be remembered, were the early days of the campaign, when the fighting was only just beginning, and when the German troops were being mobilized.

Further forward we could not go, for the French were within eight or ton miles of Saarbrucken, Forbach having only just then fallen into the hands of the Prussians, who, however, subsequently pushed on so rapidly that the enemy were soon compelled to retreat from St. Avoid, and to leave open the road between Saarbrucken and Metz. It may be asked why, when the French left this neighbourhood, we (*i.e.*, the correspondents) remained at St. Johann and Saarbrucken, where there was nothing to see. We should have been delighted to have got away, but in order to leave the town it was necessary to have the authority of the *Etappen-Commando*, who was irascible, and a *"legitimation"* from the king, who at first refused to allow correspondents to follow, or be with, his armies.

I applied to General von Göben for permission to accompany his corps, but the general was far away, and the post-offices were choked with letters. My friends who had made several applications to headquarters for *"legitimations"* were equally unlucky; not one correspondent had received a written permission at this time, and there was much discontent in consequence. Determined, however, to make a personal application at the king's *haupt-quartier*, though heaven only knew where it was situated, I resolved upon making my escape from the town on the first opportunity that presented itself.

Such a time as this was, of course, fertile of stories, and concerning the private life of the emperor everyone had something to say. The reader will remember the famous "baptism of fire" of the Prince Imperial at Saarbrucken on the 2nd of August, I give the following as it was told to me. The boy first smelt powder on the last-named day. He is said to have behaved admirably.

A bullet which fell amongst the earthworks close to him was dug out by the young prince, who with his sword cut his initials on the leaden messenger, and gave the bullet to companion as *a souvenir de la guerre*. During the fire, too, the little Napoleon made a sketch of the engagement, which much pleased the Emperor. Before closing this chapter, I should like to correct a little error into which some of the foreign correspondents fell in describing the first engagement at Saarbrucken.

I saw in many Press journals (out of which it was copied into the English papers) statements of the total destruction of Saarbrucken by the bombardment. This is so glaringly false that I wonder no one has contradicted it before. The railway station was much injured, and a few houses had bits chipped out of the walls, but that was all. The town was no more destroyed than Cologne or Mayence were, and I believe those cities have survived the war.

CHAPTER 10

Scenes in the Hospitals

Before bidding farewell to Saarbrucken, I must say something about the "Lazareth" in that town. The hospital arrangements were never better made than during the war of 1870—1. Hospitals were established in all the large cities of Germany, and especially in the frontier towns, the wounded being kept in them until they had recovered sufficiently to be taken to the permanent hospitals at Mayence, Cologne, Frankfort, &c. There were four of these "Lazareth" at Saarbrucken, and I purpose to take the reader in imagination through one of them. A large building; in point of fact, the riding-school of the Uhlans who occupy the neighbouring barracks. But ere we are well inside the building there rings in our ears a cry of anguish so acute that the blood runs cold with apprehension that a fearful crime is being committed.

Again and again comes the sound, which *anon* changes into a pitiful wail. We pass through an open door, and what do we see? A spectacle that wrings the heart. A wilderness of woe and despair. A sea of agony. "O Christ! that such things e'er could be!" Some seventy men are stretched on iron bedsteads, in all stages of suffering. A sight to make women weep and strong men shade their eyes with their hands, lest the unbidden tears should escape and proclaim their weakness "*O, Mon Dieu! Mon Dieu! Ma mere, ma mere!*" They are the cries of a French soldier—a *chasseur-à-pied*, who was shot down at the storming of the Spicherenberg. A strong, powerful fellow, the black eyes of this wounded Hercules *glimmen* (to use a poetical German word) like lode-stars. Well enough you may start and hold back, for this *chasseur* has in his right arm a hole as big as a saucer, which has been made by a rifle-bullet, and not, as you might reasonably suppose, by a shell or a round-shot.

Well enough too, he may call upon God and his mother. All jagged and torn is his arm; the blood has forced its way through shirt, and coat, and bandage, and so he shrieks again and again—"*Mon Dieu! Ma mere!*" Hold your breath; tread softly over the blankets and counterpanes which cumber the straw-littered ground; stand behind the doctor, who looks at the patient with eyes which seem to pierce through flesh and all. Here is a more serious case. This pale-faced Fransozen's leg must be amputated. The doctor has told him so, but the brave fellow is not appalled. Anything is preferable to another hour of such anguish. There are so many French wounded here that one can understand how the day went against them. What these maimed soldiers would do unless they were permitted to smoke, and had the means wherewith to gratify this taste, I do not know.

Here is a Deutscher with a gash across his head that has made him delirious. He thinks he is with his comrades in the battle-field, and imagines they are going the wrong way. "*Nein! Nein! nein!*" he shouts, until his frame trembles with excitement; his temples, on which there is a cold-water-pad, throb with agony; he starts up in bed, and it is the work of two strong men to hold him down. His eyes start from their sockets; and gleam with the light of delirium. Yet the other occupants of the "Lazareth" do not betray by word or gesture that they hear their comrade's cries. Above each man's head is written on a card his name, the number of his regiment, and the extent of his hurts. It makes the heart sick and the brain dizzy to read on almost every other card the dread word "amputation."

"*Oh! M'sieu!*" says one—he scarcely twenty, and father and mother, and little brothers and sisters, and Fauchette with the hazel eyes, litle reck of the fate that has overtaken poor Jules—"*Oh! M'sieu!* For the love of Heaven and the Saints, don't take off my leg! What will they say at home?" But you cannot avert the inevitable; and even as this poor *blessé militaire* is beseeching the surgeon to spare his limb, a delicate little instrument is at work, and, if you can bear the sight, you may witness the operation for yourself.

They must have something to read, these *verwunden* soldiers, and so on the beds you see a few books. Here is a novel of Paul de Kock's into which a priest peeps as the patient sips his coffee, and as he restores it to the pale-faced soldier a smile puckers the lips of the worthy ecclesiastic, in whose library you may be sure that volume would find no place. Paul de Kock's novel would ill consort with the *Breviary*, and the *History of the Popes*, and the theological works which crowd the priest's shelves; and I think his reverence would place the French author's story on the "Index."

The good Sisters of Mercy take care that the sick *soldaten* shall have literature of a different class to that which flowed from, the pens of Paul de Kock, Balzac, or even Dumas; thus, if you look at the bedside of this German, trooper with his right arm in a sling, you will see that he has been provided with "*Der Feld-soldaten's Freund*," a small publication issued from the press of some German printer, and which he is reading with as much interest as a Mayfair *belle* displays over the last new novel. It is right that English people should know how well these sick and suffering soldiers are cared for in the "Lazareth."

Coffee, meat, eggs, wine, bread, butter, cherry-brandy, and, anything more that the wisdom of the doctors and nurses may prescribe, are found within the hospital walls; and all these nourishments are dispensed by the loving hands of ladies, who, *malgré* the fact that hitherto they have been unused to such scenes of misery as those which now present themselves, yet show a tact which is nothing less than marvellous in administering drugs and applying bandages. It is seldom given to Englishmen to see the working of the Continental system of relief to the wounded in time of war. I had an opportunity of witnessing the scheme in all its ramifications, and it is not too much to say that the plan was the most perfect that could be adopted.

Everyone took part in it—Roman Catholic priest, Lutheran clergy, Sisters of Mercy, monks of the Benedictine and Franciscan Orders, and civilians. Every lady who was engaged in the grand work—and there were very few who did not lend their assistance—wore upon her arm the red cross upon a white ground, which was the emblem of her charitable profession. These helpers all gave of their substance to the Lazareth, the cost of which was consequently scarcely felt by the Government. But the Lazareth, spacious as they were, could not hold all the wounded, many of whom were billeted upon private families; and, during the months of August and September particularly, many of the frontier towns in Germany were no more nor less than gigantic hospitals, almost every house having its quota of *verwunden*.

I witnessed some very touching incidents in the Lazareth. An old peasant who had tramped into Saarbrucken all the way from Lebach, came in search of his son, who he feared had been wounded in the storming of the Spicherenberg on the 6th of August. He entered one of the Lazareth, and inquired for his child. The Sisters of Charity looked all round the wards, but the boy was not there. "Like enough," said an artilleryman, whose leg had been amputated on the previous day, "like enough he lies at Bellevue," where now repose so many of the dead, a little wooden cross indicating the last resting-place of many a gallant German and Frenchman.

During my stay at St. Johann, I visited, in company with a distinguished member of the Society of Jesus, the barracks of the Uhlans, which also had been converted into a "Lazareth." Here were two French officers and a sergeant, who had been, wounded in the storming of the Spicherenberg. During the time I was conversing with these gentlemen, a youth came in, accompanied by a boy-friend, and asked if his father (a French, officer) was in the "Lazareth." They had come from Paris to look for the missing parent, of whom they could get no information. The poor boy's eyes filled with tears when he was told that his father was not in the hospital, and he left us with a heavy heart to renew his dismal quest.

CHAPTER 11

An Escape from Saarbrucken

There was at every considerable German town, and at every French town occupied by the Prussians, an official possessed of absolute authority, known as the *Etappen-Commando*, or commandant, as we should call him. The gentleman who filled this office at Saarbrucken was fully impressed with the weight of his position He had, moreover, so great a dislike to newspaper correspondents that he refused to let any of us leave the town by railway unless we were already provided with the magic "*legitimation*," which, at this time, nobody had received—nobody, I should say, with the exception of a gentleman who represented a Vienna journal.

Wishing to go forward without further delay, I took counsel with that fortunate gentleman, and the result of our discussion was that I resolved to make an endeavour to escape from the sway of the despotic commandant. Hastily packing up one morning we left the Rheinischer Hof for the railway-station where the eagle glance of the commandant was fixed inquiringly on us—the more so as our knapsacks were strapped on, and our bags and field-glasses slung. We mooned about the long platform with an indifferent air, sauntered by the commandant, gravely saluted that monarch *pro tem.*, and, hearing that a train was at this moment starting—had, in fact, started—for Remilly, near Metz, cunningly made our way through a labyrinth of trucks, jumped on the steps of the guards' van as the train was going and, in two minutes, had left St. Johann station and the despotic commandant far behind.

We passed Styring and Forbach, the first French towns you see after leaving Saarbrucken. Both manufacturing towns; but the war had driven away employers and artisans, the sounds of labour were no more heard, the tall-chimnied factories were silent, and only a few Prussian and French wounded soldiers looked out of the windows as we steamed by. War showed its grim face at every step. The delays *en route* were, as may be supposed, terribly frequent. We waited at St. Avold (which until a few days before had been the French headquarters) for ten hours, and, as night approached, the soldiers made large fires along the line, and were soon regaling themselves with soup and coffee. We stopped seventeen times at Faulquemont, where the Prussians had seized an immense Government tobacco manufactory, and confiscated its contents.

The scenes at Remilly were indescribably painful. I witnessed few spectacles more dreadful all through the campaign. Our train pulled up at some distance from the station, and when we walked to the platform, we found it thronged by wounded men in every stage of agony. These were the men who had suffered at Gorze on the 18th of August. Shot through the eyes, in the head, in the face, legs, chest, and arms; there, in the chill air, with no covering but straw to protect them from rain and wind, lay the flower of the German armies. Women, and girls, and men were binding up their wounds by the uncertain, ever-decreasing light of evening, and although train after train was dispatched, it seemed as if they would never cease bringing in the wounded soldiers. In rude carts and uncomfortable waggons, on hand litters borne by German students or peasants, came these suffering beings, all red with blood, and faint with the heat and burden of the day.

I never saw men with such fearful wounds as these German soldiers on the platform at Remilly. It will be remembered that when the *mitrailleuse* first brought into notice, everybody marvelled at the completeness of this instrument of death, and that subsequently the French invention was scoffed and sneered at.

People said, "Oh, the *mitrailleur,* or *mitrailleuse,* or whatever it is called, only be used on level ground. After all, it is but forty rifles secured on one stock by bands. It is not so very 'formidable.' True, it killed 300 horses at one discharge at Châlons; but then the poor animals were all fastened together, and could not move." There was much more to the same effect; and, later, it was said that the Prussians who had these *mitrailleuses,* which had done great execution in a certain battle—Wörth, I think, was named.

Of course, that was a mistake; but the greatest error was made by the persons who undervalued, or rather underestimated, the power of the *mitrailleuse.* It was the *"mitrailleuse"* which caused the greater portion of the losses at Gorze. It was the same murderous weapon which mowed down the ranks of the Prussians at Wörth and Weissemburg, and which was so destructive at the Battle of Saarbrucken. Do you ask how this man got that awful wound in the face, how that one came to be so cut and slashed across his bead, and how his comrade escaped with life after receiving that tremendous gash in the neck? I answer, it was the *mitrailleuse.* You need not seek for corroboration of this statement; it is written down from the lips of the Germans themselves. The *mitrailleuse* was the terrible "sensation" weapon of the War!

But whilst the platform at Remilly was crowded with the wounded, outside the station, in the large place, the sight was more appalling still. By the sides of the houses and the station railings, under carts, and waggons, and trees, were lying hundreds of sufferers, and the "Lazareth" which had been hastily "run up" was full. There were many willing hands to bind up their wounds—amongst them a pioneer band from London.—but they were as sands of the sea amongst so many. Uncomplaining, many so badly hurt that their recovery was impossible, these sick *soldaten* at Remilly made up a picture which only Gustave Doré's powerful pencil could adequately reproduce.

Remilly, then, being a small town, all unused to the horrors of war, and to having its houses of entertainment metamorphosed into "Lazareth," was problematical whether two travellers alighting at its station a few hours after the battle of Gorze would find food and shelter within its boundaries; and, this being so, it became the two travellers to immediately seek for both. They did so in a very practical manner. Remilly has many hotels, *cafés*, and restaurants, such as they are; but they were all closed. Remilly has also a tolerable number of shops, but they, too, had the shutters up, and gave no signs of life, save in one instance, and that was where a German Jew—a short man, with a sallow face, and little black eyes that twinkled like live coals—had opened the shop of someone who had fled, and was selling cigars at a very handsome profit.

We tried one house after the other, and were in every case sent empty away. Night was advancing, and there seemed every prospect of our passing the night in the open heaven's blue canopy our only blanket, when Providence threw in our way a kindly-disposed sergeant of infantry. More used to foraging in war times than we were, our *militaire*, in the course of a walk through the streets of Remilly, entertained us with a recital of recent events, promised he would find us a bed in the house where he and his men were quartered, and, in the midst of a conversation, suddenly left us, saying "he wanted to speak to a comrade respecting our supper." We marvelled, and walked slowly on.

A minute afterwards there was a loud cackling of ducks, which a soldier in undress uniform was pursuing, apparently with feelings the reverse of friendly. Thinking it had escaped, a fat duck, which was old enough to have known better, was slowly waddling through a pool by the side of the road, when the same soldier who had previously betokened the interest he took in this useful bird, approached with stealthy steps, and dealt the silly thing a blow on the head, which knocked it lifeless on the ground. A *gamin* in a blue blouse, yelling horribly, meantime gave chase to and captured another duck, and, amid the shrieks of its owner, an aged and garrulous female, gave it into the hands of our soldier-friend, who, waving the quacking biped on high, bade us follow him.

In company of some score of others, soldiers, *gamins*, &c., we did follow, and were just in time to witness the decapitation of the duck, a deed performed with one blow of a sword. That duck, which had been thus hastily offered up as a sacrifice to the god Mars, furnished two Special Correspondents with the first and only repast placed before them that day. It was cooked the garden of the Hotel et Café de France, where two soldiers had made a fire of whatever they could lay their hands on; and, with the aid of a flask of red wine and, some brown bread, we supped with an appetite sharpened by twenty-four hours' abstinence. We slept in the apartment but lately sacred to *Table d'Hôte,* but now appropriated by the Prussians as a sleeping-room. In this chamber were twenty-two gentlemen who had adopted the profession of arms.

We were consequently twenty-four in a room about eighteen feet by nine. We all slept on straw strewed on the floor, and I think I never more enjoyed a night's rest. In the morning—it was Sunday, I the way—we rose at five o'clock, and made our *toilette* at a pump in the street, using pocket-handkerchiefs for towels; and, after hastily swallowing some very bitter coffee and some more brown-black bread, we went off to the station to take another look at the wounded (who were even at that early hour being sent off by rail to Saarbrucken), as well as to obtain a vehicle which would take us to Pont-à-Mousson, concerning which there was considerable difficulty.

Having procured a waggon without springs, a horse half-dead from fatigue, and a driver who had lost his head at sight of so much soldiery, we left Remilly, with its deserted houses—and there are some very fine mansions with beautiful gardens there—and, if I may use a nautical phrase, "*crowded all sail*" for Pont-à-Mousson, in the province of Lorraine.

The train which took us to Remilly conveyed a party of English ladies and gentlemen belonging to the Society for the Belief of the Wounded in War, whose offices were at St. Martin's Place. This party—a pioneer detachment, as they told me—was composed of five ladies and three gentlemen, the former wearing an uniform consisting of close-fitting gray dresses, with hats and jackets of the same colour, and all displaying the Geneva cross on their sleeves and on their hats. I am glad to be able to bear witness to the usefulness of the English party, who did good service to my knowledge at Faulquemont and Remilly, where I lost sight of them.

CHAPTER 12

The Bombardment of Toul

Leaving Remilly, we passed, on our way to Pont-à-Mousson, through a country desolated and nearly deserted. Every house in every village and town we rode through was closed; the few people who had not fled on the approach of the Prussians stood at their doors and regarded us sullenly; it was as though a pestilence had come upon the country and decimated the population. The people told us, in answer to our demand for something to eat, that the Prussians had taken everything; and it was certain that the invading armies had swept like a dark cloud over the provinces, seizing all they could find, never dreaming of paying for what they took, nor thinking that those wretched peasants were thus placed on the brink of starvation. I neither saw nor heard of any atrocities being committed by the Prussians, who, provided they could get a sufficiency to eat and drink, behaved exceedingly well. Everywhere between Remilly and Pont-à-Mousson we saw the German soldiers making railways—one to circumvent Metz—and laying down the field-telegraph, the thin black-and-white poles of which you could trace for miles.

Pont-à-Mousson was full of Germans. On the day of our arrival there the king had made it his headquarters, and it was there that I saw His Majesty for the first time. I was looking at the troops who were bivouacked in the market-place, where fires were burning, and cooking was going on, when there was a rush to one side of the place, and a cry that the king was there. I hurried across the road, and there, in front of the Hotel de Ville, was *der König*—a tall, handsome, gray-bearded, soldierly-looking old gentleman, with a benevolent smile perpetually playing about his mouth. King William is essentially a *soldier*. Eschewing all the pomp and panoply which most sovereigns deem it necessary to indulge in, the King of Prussia rarely has a larger staff with him than one of his generals possesses. Often, indeed, he rides about unaccompanied, save by one gentleman. When I saw him in August, at Pont-à-Mousson, he was speaking to some officers, who, as is their wont, kept their right arm at the salute whilst in the presence of the king. His Majesty, however, does not care for this sort of homage, and in each case good-humouredly "knocked down" the arm of the officer who was addressing him. A simple liver, a thorough soldier, and an urbane gentleman, the king is beloved by his troops, who see in him the man who has made Germany a foremost military nation of the earth.

At Pont-à-Mousson, amongst many other notabilities—Members of the Landtag &c.—I met Colonel Corvin, whom I may describe as a cosmopolitan journalist. He was acting as war correspondent for an English paper, for the German *Gartenlauber*, for the Vienna *Neue Frie Presse*, and for another German *zeitung*. From him I learnt of the sad death of Prince Salm-Salm and his nephew, who fell side by side at the Battle of Gorze. Prince Salm, whose adventurous career was thus brought to a premature conclusion, will be remembered as the biographer of the unfortunate Emperor Maximilian. He had wandered all over Europe and through a good deal of America in search of excitement, and when the Franco-German war broke out he applied to the King of Prussia for a commission, which he received.

His nephew—a mere boy—was made the prince's *aide-de-camp*. The Battle of Gorze was almost their first engagement, and both fell, fighting side by aide. It was a sad story, and my narrator's eyes filled with tears in the telling of it; for he had known both prince and princess intimately for many years. The Princess Salm, who is the daughter of English parents, has been of the greatest assistance throughout the war, acting at nurse, and inspiring all around her by her courage and usefulness. During the king's brief visit to Saarbrucken His Majesty met the princess carrying a bucket of water in one hand and a of soup in the other! His Majesty had a long interview with the heroic lady, and highly complimented her upon her conduct. The prince died a poor man, but I understand that the Queen of Prussia (with whom the Princess Salm is a deservedly great favourite) has provided for the brave lady to an extent commensurate with her high position in society.

The three battles of Borny, Gravelotte, and Mars-la-Tour, which were fought on the 14th, 16th, and 18th of August, were the bloodiest series of engagements during the campaign. That on the 18th of August, and which the Germans call the Battle of Gorze, from a large village of that name near which the fighting took place, resulted in at least 50,000 men being killed and wounded. The battlefield was the most awful sight that can be imagined. The scene of the conflict was a cluster of villages, of which Gorze is the principal, although that place itself was hardly concerned in the fight of the 18th.

The carnage was awful. Everywhere the dead were piled up in large heaps, the flies crawling over their pallid faces and bloodstained uniforms. Horses shot down by *chassepôts* and needle-guns, their wounds gaping in the morning sun, lay in all attitudes, with men upon and under them. Here was a Prussian infantryman, his countenance all livid and distorted by the agony of the death-wound which laid him low; next to him reposed, in the calm indifference of death, a young lieutenant, who had dreamt of glory, and fame, and honours, maybe, and who had found instead a grave on the enemy's soil. You could tell he died as he was hopefully leading on his company, for a smile was on his lips yet.

From his breast-pocket peeped the corner of a letter—a dainty pink note, which haply contained his sweetheart' sprayers for his safety. Attached to a little locket was a piece of sunny, golden hair; and you might be sure that that ring of amethysts and pearls which he wears was given him in the happy peace-times under the lindens. The *mitrailleuses* had once more done terrible mischief. I saw several men with half their heads blown away, with one leg taken clean off, with an arm separated from the body as neatly as though it had been, amputated by a surgeon. There were some fearful breast-wounds too—wounds that gaped horribly, and made one sick to look at.

Where the *mitrailleuse* had been brought into operation, there were heaps of Prussian dead, hundreds piled around each other—a ghastly sight to see. Close to a Prussian artilleryman was a French officer, a captain of *chasseurs*, stricken by a bullet from a needle-gun, his eyes wide open, his mouth tightly closed, as though he had died cursing his antagonists. Not far from the little hill where the French artillery had made such a long at was the body of a trumpeter, a mere lad, whom it was surely a sin and a shame to send into the battlefield. The ground was a vast mass dead and dying. Your boots were tinged with the life-blood of many a gallant fellow ere you had walked three yards. Hecatombs of dead, heaps of dying, met the gaze everywhere. It was easy enough, if you had the courage and the patience to wade through the carnage, to see which regiments had suffered most.

Those Prussian regiments which lost most men were the 2nd, 3rd, 8th, 9th, 10th, 11th, 12th, 14th, 16th, 20th, 21st, 22nd, 24th, 28th, 29th, 33rd, 35th, 36th, 40th, 42nd, 43rd, 44th, 48th, 49th, 52nd, 54th, 55th, 56th, 57th, 60th, 64th, 67th, 69th, 72nd, 74th. 76th, 77th, 79th, 85th, 91st, 105th, and 107th.

All these regiments suffered severely. On the French side the infantry sustained the greatest losses, whilst the casualties amongst the artillery and *chasseurs*; were also very considerable. There were many marvellous escapes on both sides. An officer of Prussian infantry showed me a rent made in his jacket by the bullet from a *chassepôt*, which had. gone straight along his chest, taking off one of the buttons of his tunic. Many had perforations through the little spike at the apex of their helmets, and others were shot through the cuffs of their coats. Altogether, the battle was the bloodiest in the history of the war, and resulted in Bazaine and his "*Armée du Rhin*" being entirely cut off from Paris. It was the soldiers wounded at Borny, Gravelotte, and Mar-la-

Tour whom I had seen at Remilly, and met between Remilly and Pont-à-Mousson; and it was near the latter place that I saw 6,000 French prisoners, resting by the wayside under charge of a very few Prussian soldiers.

The king moved his headquarters so rapidly that it was extremely difficult to keep up with him. I was following the staff to Commercy when I heard that there had been a great battle near Toul. I accordingly made off in that direction as rapidly as possible. From Pont-à-Mousson to Toul is thirty-five miles, but the roads being exceedingly good—long *chaussées*, straight as an arrow, extending as the crow flies sometimes for four or five miles—I reached it early in the day, and after a careful reconnaissance, in view of the enemy being rumoured to be in the neighbourhood, obtained an interview with a Bavarian officer from whom I learnt that there had been no battle but a bombardment of an extensive character.

Toul, which is delightfully situated in a valley and has a grand old cathedral, had refused to surrender when called upon to do so, and, being a strong fortress, declined to listen to any terms of capitulation. The Bavarians consequently took their guns to the top of the hills surrounding Toul, and commenced to bombard it. The Bavarian grenades struck the cathedral, and set a large storehouse on fire; and the commandant replied by a vigorous cannonade. This was the "great battle" reported to have been fought, The cannonade had caused the greatest fright to the inhabitants of the villages within twelve or fifteen miles of Toul, the terrified people imagining that the Prussians were much nearer to them than in reality they were. I returned to Pont-à-Mousson the same night, after being stopped once or twice by the foreposts, who had lit large fires in the road, and in a rickyard near Pont-à-Mousson; and the next day I left for Commercy, the new headquarters of the king.

Chapter 13

From Commercy to Clermont

From the 18th of August to the 29th was not a very stirring time. There had been some small engagements—at Jarny, for instance, where the Chasseurs d'Afrique had put some Uhlans to flight—but nothing that attracted much notice at the king's headquarters. With my Austrian friend I visited the *haupt-quartier* two or three times a day in quest of news; the answer we usually received was, "*Nichts neues dieser Tag.*" We could receive no newspapers or letters at this time, for we were "unattached," and never knew where we should be two days together. Occasionally, however, we found a German or French journal lying about, and from that source we gathered what had transpired in other parts of the country which had been so successfully invaded by the German forces.

The day after my visit to Toul I left Pont-à-Mousson—which was full of troops, "Johanniters," *marktenters*, and representatives of various Ambulance Corps—for Commercy, where the king had established his headquarters. I now saw, in all its full reality, the result of the German occupation of these eastern districts of France. In nearly every town and village I passed through, with the exception of Pont-à-Mousson and Bar-le-Duc, the shopkeepers had closed their places of business the *cafés* were *fermé*, and all trade at a standstill. The few people I saw were sullen and depressed; no children played in the streets or fields; it was a desolate country where the German soldiers were not bivouacked.

As for the French soldiers, they were never seen, save as prisoners. There was not the slightest resistance to the advance of the Prussian regiments, many of which made forced marches in view of a great future movement, the plan evidently being to drive the enemy towards the Belgian frontier, as was indeed the ease. The country appeared to be mourning for some departed great one of the earth. The general depression was intense. At Commercy, the suburbs of which have quite a home-look, I found a few soldiers, who were under orders to go forward on the following day.

The king had left on the morning of my arrival for Bar-le-Duc. The streets of Commercy were deserted, save by the military; the Prussian black-and-white standard waved from the public buildings; and, side by side, on the walls of the Hotel de Ville were French placards headed *"Subscription en faveur de l'armée,"* and King William's printed announcement, *"La Conscription est abolie dans toute l'entendue du territoire Français occupé par les troupes Allemandes."* The Prussians were most sanguine as to the future. "We shall be in Paris in fourteen days from now" (August 24), said some Prussian officers to me at *table d'hôte*; and I thought of the prediction three months later, when I was *"vor Paris"* with the same gentlemen.

At Bar-le-Duc—a large, handsome town, with a long *boulevard* running through it—there was a large force of Prussians, who had arrived two days before—*viz.*, on the 23rd of August. They signalized their entry by seizing all the letters at the post-office, demanding 150 rations, 300 horse-shoes, and 50,000 *francs* (£2,000)! They received everything but the money, which it was impossible to give them, the bank having sent all its valuables to Paris on the previous day. I remained at Bar-le-Duc only one night, being anxious to keep near the king, whose headquarters had been again pushed on to Clermont, which I reached on the 27th of August.

When you enter a strange town in the middle of the night, as I did, in company with two doctors of the *Sanitaats* corps, your ideas of locality and surroundings are of rather a vague description; and you go to bed, dreaming that you hear the roll of the drums, the shrill piping of the fifes, the loud blasts of the trumpets, and other martial music—all of which sounds were in my ears as I stretched my weary limbs, cramped by a fifteen hours' ride, on the heap of straw which did duty for a bed here, as in, alas! too many other places which I had visited since the last week in July. This being so, I was surprised on the following morning to find the town large and picturesque. Clermont is built on the top of a hill.

We took forcible possession of the first house we came to "in the name of the King," who, I am sure, would have approved our mode of procedure. As the streets of Clermont are at present, climbing the steep ascent to the town proper is a task of considerable difficulty—for, although the highways are all macadamized, yet a whole night's rain makes them ankle-deep in a white mud, which sticks as close to your trousers and boots as the preserve does to an *omelette confiture*. The one long street, with its few avenues, was a mass of this white mud. Each side of the way was lined with baggage waggons and officers' carriages, and on every house were chalk indications that soldiers were billeted there.

The Town Post Office was changed into a "field police office," having for its chef one of the pleasantest silver-haired officials I ever met; *haupt-quartiers* were everywhere; and at No. 21 in the main thoroughfare were the apartments of His Majesty the King of Prussia, overlooked by the church, which is on another hill in the middle of the town, and which you ascend by something like 100 steps. No. 21 is by no means a "swell" sort of house; it: plain white building, opposite a stable and coach-house, and nothing like so grand a residence as His Majesty had at Saarbrucken. There was no flag flying—nothing to denote the king's presence save two helmeted soldiers A Bavarian Army Corps had been in bivouac outside the town; and I was fortunate enough to witness their departure.

At eight a.m. the first battalion marched through Clermont, their splendid band of forty-three men playing the "*Sardannepal Marrsch*" (the march from *Sardanapalus*). As they went by No.

21, the king appeared at the open window. You could see how proud he is of his soldiers—of the Bavarians especially, for many of these men come from those portions of Bavaria which Prussia amalgamated in the North German Confederation after Sadowa. Amongst all the 37,803,012 people from whom Germany takes her soldiers, better men could not be found than these Bavarian *Jägers* and *Chevaux-légers*. As they marched under the windows of the house No. 21, the casement was thrown open, and the venerable King of Prussia appeared, and gravely saluted the captain each company with a nod of the head. "*Hoch! hoch! hoch!*" came from the men—not with that regularity which marks the cheering of our own soldiers, not spontaneously down the whole line, but fitfully, and only from the heads of companies.

The order was "eyes left" until the battalion had passed the king's apartments, and every man had seen *der König*. The last cheers had scarcely died away ere the arrival of another battalion of Bavarians was announced. The king commanded the battalion to halt. Some of the officers were presented to His Majesty, who came out in the pouring rain and stood chatting to his officers as though it were an ordinary review-day and the weather charming. This brave old soldier (he is 74) was dressed like any other general officer in his army—tunic and trousers of blue, a spiked helmet, low boots, and a cloak thrown over his shoulders to protect, him from the rain, of which, however, he took no heed The only ornament he wore was the blue-and-gold star which you see under the neck of every general in the Prussian army. The king had no other decorations.

After several officers had been presented to him in front of the royal headquarters, the king requested that all the other officers of the battalion might be made known to him. His Majesty was accordingly conducted down the line, and all the officers were called to the front. As each gentleman's name was mentioned by the officer in command of the regiment, the king made the customary salute until forty or fifty officers had been presented. His Majesty then briefly addressed them. It was the shortest speech I ever reported. Here it is:-

Meine Herren,—I am very much pleased to see the troops of Bavaria with those of Prussia. It has also given me a great deal of pleasure to observe the bravery you have displayed and the zeal you possess. I hope that this unity of all the German armies will long remain as it is, and that you will get yet more glory.

During the time he was speaking, the king's face was suffused by a sunny smile, and his manner showed how delighted he was with his army, and how sanguine as to the ultimate result of the war. After this little ceremony His Majesty returned to his lodgings, and stood in the street opposite whilst the third battalion marched past. At a little distance were General von Moltke and two or three other officers, and in attendance on the king was Herr von Alten. The king's *aide-de-camp* is a splendid specimen of a soldier, and a remarkably handsome man. His sister is the Duchess of Manchester, whose noble husband was with the Prussians for a considerable period during the early stages of the war.

A prominent spectator of this little incident at Clermont was General Sheridan, of the United States Army, whom I also saw a week later at the Battle of Sedan. General Sheridan is about the average height, rather stout, with a pleasant face that the sun has made as brown as a backwoodsman's, jet-black moustache, and twinkling eyes. He was dressed in black, and wore a jacket with brass buttons—the only conspicuous point in his costume. With him were two American friends—the most genuine Americans that can be imagined. The scenes in the streets that day were amusing enough. There was, as there always is, a great rush for provisions in the morning, and the solitary shop which was open, set up by an enterprising German, by the way, for the occasion, was besieged.

I went in to buy whatever I could get, for one is not particular in war times, and found a general, a colonel, and several under-officers and men, bargaining for *schinken*, sausage, wine, and cigars. The general marched off triumphantly with a large ham, which cost him twelve *thalers*. Others were supplied on a smaller scale, and all the edibles in the store were disposed of in a few minutes. I noticed General Moltke going across the street, from the headquarters to his lodgings, with a huge sausage in one hand, and his sword in the other, and two other generals saw and envied him.

There was now a general march forward of Bavarians and Prussians, and I followed the next move of the royal headquarters. On the 28th of August I reached Varennes, and heard that an outpost engagement had taken place at Buzancy, and that there had been a sharp skirmish between Uhlans and some men of the 48th (French) regiment. These were but the preliminaries to the great battles at Beaumont and Sedan. At Varennes (where I had the pleasure of meeting Mr. Sutherland Edwards, one of the correspondents of *The Times*—the first English face I had seen for many weeks) I slept at the Hotel du Grand Monarque, a tavern of historical repute. On the bridge which crosses the turbid stream close by, Louis XIV. was captured after his flight from Paris; and the hotel has been visited by all the literary notabilities of the last half century.

CHAPTER 14

An Alarm at Buzancy

Leaving Varennes soon after daybreak on Tuesday, August 30, I little thought that within forty-eight hours I should witness the two most important battles of the war, and see Napoleon III. and his army of 90,000 men surrender themselves as prisoners to the King of Prussia! It was not until we had been three hours on the road leading to Buzancy, Beaumont, and Sedan, that the Prussian troops were visible. At 1 p.m. I was at Buzancy. The town was full of German troops, and there was great excitement. I was searching for some lunch at a small tavern, when, hearing a clatter of horses' feet and carriages, I ran into the street and was just in time to get out of the way of a battery of Bavarian artillery, which galloped by at a furious pace. Other batteries followed; infantry came rapidly up; sounds of a cannonade were faintly heard.

At this time a Prussian officer informed me that he had made a reconnaissance of the French troops that morning, and that there were not more than 120,000 in all, while the Prussians had eight Army Corps of 30,000 men each! This was a slight error, as I subsequently ascertained that the total strength of the French in the neighbourhood of Sedan was upwards of 130,000. There was no doubt that a battle was being fought, and I and my friends hurried on with all possible speed towards the front. We had hardly got outside the town ere we found ourselves in the midst of several thousand Bavarians, who were making a forced march. Look where you would from this position (we were on rising ground beyond Buzancy) soldiers were visible scattered over a glorious landscape.

There was a light breeze, and a fierce sun, which glinted on masses of bayonets and swords. Along a winding, uphill road, through a pool of water, and then over hills of Buzancy we went with the Bavarian *soldaten*. The road was dotted with wine-bottles; in one place I noticed a man's tall hat—a "topper" that might have been made by Christie; all along the *chaussée* were soldiers, obliged to fall out owing to fatigue—some seated on the banks, others lying prone on the ground, who might have said with Mr. Tennyson's heroine—

"*I am aweary, aweary. I would that I were dead.*"

It was a wonderfully beautiful picture—two church spires miles away; a vast extent cultivated land—hill, and valley, and plain; soldiers everywhere; and the blue sky, flecked with white clouds, looking down upon all. At half-past two we saw the smoke of cannons miles in front of as, just as we were within a *kilométre* of Vaux-en-Dieulet, where there was an encampment of 100,000 French troops. These formed the greater part of the army of Marshal MacMahon, With them was the emperor. Sniffing the battle from afar, all the German troops forgot their fatigue, and, throwing away their boots in many instances, marched quickly forward, although many regiments had been on foot all night.

In front of us was the king's carriage, in which was seated Prince Friedrich Karl. We were now within seven *kilométres* of Beaumont, where, on the previous day, the Saxons. 60,000 in number, had surprised General de Failly's *corps d'armée*, who were cleaning their rifles and cooking. De Failly had been guilty of the crime—for his neglect amounted to a crime—of not putting any foreposts out. Thousands of prisoners were taken by the Prussians after an engagement lasting several hours, during which those of the French not cut to pieces or taken prisoners made a hurried retreat across the Meuse, leaving on the field many cannon and *mitrailleuses*. Several hours before our arrival at Vaux the Saxons, Prussians, and the First Bavarian Corps had again attacked what remained of the army corps of De Failly and the French troops to whom I have referred as being encamped at Vaux.

It was five o'clock before we reached Beaumont and had taken up our position on the hills before Raucourt. For half an hour not a French soldier was visible, although we heard cannonading and rifle-shooting at some distance. Suddenly a small body of the enemy appeared in front, and at once began a smart fire with their *chassepôts*. The Bavarian infantry replied without loss of time. Advancing in skirmishing order, they opened a rapid fire upon the enemy, whose artillery, which we had not before observed, now commenced. Already in position, the "Bayern" cannon poured grenade after grenade, shrapnel after shrapnel, into the ranks of the Fransozens.

Advancing with the Bavarian infantry, I found myself between two fires, with no more shelter than that afforded by some small heaps of earth. The skirmishers were lying flat on the ground, the fire from the enemy being very severe; and, finding that the *chassepôt* bullets were falling much too close to be pleasant, and that the French shells were increasing in number, I threw myself on the earth and waited the course of events. When the firing slackened a little, I walked forward a few paces, observed the relative positions of the contending forces, and then withdrew to the positions occupied by the Bavarian artillery, one battery of six guns being on one hill, and a second battery placed opposite. It was dark before the last shot was fired, but before that the French were retreating in the direction of Sedan.

Darkness set in so quickly whilst I was looking about the battlefield, that I felt like a Babe in the Wood. The country was unknown to me, the darkness increased every moment; and artillery and cavalry were flying along the road to the peril of all wayfarers. The Bavarians went into bivouac immediately after the engagement; and soon had fires blazing all over the hills and in the valley. I took shelter in a cottage which had only been just quitted by its inhabitants, who had left everything behind them;

some—probably the aged and decrepit—had evidently risen from their beds a few minutes before I entered the house, for the beds were still warm. Faint with hunger, thirst, and fatigue, I looked about me for something *à manger*, but could find nothing. Acting, however, upon a happy thought, I dragged a blanket from a bed, and underneath the mattress, to my unspeakable delight, I found a large loaf, which I shared with the *soldaten*.

More than 100 bottles of wine were discovered by those industrious troopers in the cellar, besides two or three large barrels of Burgundy. After this frugal repast I lit my candle—for no prudent correspondent ever travels without one—and, making a desk of a couple of chairs, began to write my narrative of the battle and its incidental scenes. Curious to a fault, the "Bayerns" watched my movements from beginning to end, unable to comprehend what they evidently regarded as the vagaries of an "*Englander*."

The bed I had selected was monopolized by two Bavarian soldiers, who snored with exceeding regularity, *malgré* the severe shaking to which I subjected them. I awoke at daylight and looked at the strange scene before me. A silver-gray mist hung over every object; the bivouac-fires were burning redly even then; occasionally the sound of a distant bugle was wafted through the slumbering air; and presently there was a movement in the bivouc, horses' feet were heard, and then the onward march of the troops began.

Chapter 15

A Days Rest at Raucourt

The morning of the 31st of August saw some 200,000 men on the march. Raucourt, a small town near Beaumont, was the rendezvous of several thousand German soldiers, who had no, idea that the great affair at Beaumont would be so quickly followed by the greater victory at Sedan. Early in the morning I entered Raucourt with the troops, who were in the highest spirits, having apparently recovered the severe fatigue of forced marches and bivouacs in the rain for several nights together. The Fourth Army Corps was in bivouac for twenty-eight successive nights, during most of which period rain fell in torrents. Yet they were as fresh at the end of August as they were a month earlier, when they left Magdeburg for France.

During engagement on the 30th, I had missed my journalistic friends of London and Vienna, who had slept at Raucourt, and whom I found the next morning at an hotel in earnest conversation with General ———. My Vienna friend was exploding with wrath. His "*legitimation*" given him by General von Podbielski, to whose kindness I was also indebted for my permission to roam wherever I pleased. General ———, however, had refused to allow any correspondents to proceed farther than Raucourt, though he gave no reason for this order. This so incensed the Vienna journalist that he "flew at" both the general and his *aide-de camp* with such fury that the little *Ritmeister* demanded an apology, which was ultimately tendered and courteously received.

The prohibition of the general was not enforced at all events it was not heeded by at least three correspondents. The Hotel de Ville at Raucourt was converted into a "Lazareth," from the windows of which the French wounded looked wistfully out at the crowd which filled the little streets—officers, priests, soldiers, townsfolk, *sanitaats*-men, and journalists picking up crumbs of information of the Battle of Beaumont. There was absolutely nothing to eat at Raucourt. The shops had been sacked—shamefully pillaged in truth—by the Prussians, whose conduct was in many eases reprehensible. Not content with taking what was serviceable, the soldiers utterly wrecked the mercers', grocers', and bootmakers' shops, each trying to outvie the other in the extent of mischief.

At the hotels you were unable to purchase anything; and it was only by going from house to house, explaining that I was not a Prussian, and absolutely begging for bread and milk, that I was enabled to buy sufficient to sustain me. Observing the doors of the church open, I entered. An extraordinary scene presented itself. The building was full of soldiers, eating, and drinking, and singing. Their rifles, swords, and helmets were thrown about recklessly. Some were on the altar, the white frontal of which had been torn to tatters, and the sacred paraphernalia cast on the ground. The little shrines at each side of the church were turned into receptacles for munitions of war, and the whole interior was as if a band of Hottentots had entered the place and desecrated it.

Outside the town, on, the road to Sedan, the French had encamped on, the day preceding the Battle of Beaumont. Compelled to retreat hurriedly, as was almost invariably the case, they had left on the ground all that they could not conveniently carry away. The grass was strewn with knapsacks, *chassepôts*, cartridges, caps, and linen; scattered about were hundreds of letters—letters from mothers and sisters to sons and brothers, from friends to friends, from sweethearts to sweethearts—letters of earnest hope that the war would soon be over; others entreating Jules or Adolphe to return so soon as they bad driven the Prussians out of the country; others breathing warm words of unchangeable love. It was a melancholy spectacle, this bivouac, with everything telling of bitter humiliation and death.

During the battle of the 30th, *grenaden* and rifle-bullets had fallen into the French camp, killing both men and horses. The former had been buried; the latter were lying on the ground, their bodies swollen and their eyes staring. In the evening, after dark, I paid a second visit to the locality. How changed the scene! The spot had been chosen by the Bavarians for their bivouac. Fires were blazing on both sides of the road; the men were preparing their suppers; others were asleep, wrapped in their thick dark-grey coats; and not a few were enjoying the unusual luxury of sleeping under canvas—the canvas tents which the Fransozens had left behind.

Although the result of the Battle of Beaumont was to fill all the "Lazareth" with wounded French and German soldiers, there was no lack of medical assistance. At Raucourt I found several gentlemen connected with the International Ambulance Corps. Amongst others were Mr. H. A. Blount, of Paris, well known in England for his skill as an amateur steeple-chase rider; and the Comte de Ganay. From these gentlemen I learnt that the battle had been productive of most fatal consequences to the French, compelling them to retreat towards Belgium. The inhabitants of Raucourt were greatly terrified at the firing, and it is a fact that one poor old man fell dead in the street from fear! A French soldier became crazed from the same cause.

Boom! A pause for a second—then another report deeper than the first; then another another, then a fifth, followed by a succession of cannon-shots; an ocean of white smoke in the hot, still air; and then a furious cannonade, repeated again and again! These were the first indications I had of the Battle of Sedan, on the 1st of September. I had left Raucourt with my Vienna friend, at half-past seven that morning, determined to get as far forward as I could. A mile out of the town, having occasion to speak to a soldier, who was standing amidst a heap of broken *chassepôts*, I was told that by going on a little farther we should come to a battlefield.

On that occasion neither of us had a horse; so, sometimes running and sometimes walking, we pushed on rapidly, encountering some artillerymen returning at a gallop for ammunition. Just beyond Hauraucourt we saw the battle raging at some two or three miles' distance. At Angecourt a battery of artillery was at that moment going forward, and we got a seat on one of the baggage waggons, dismounting only when the press of infantry in front made speedy progress impossible. Jumping off the waggon, then, and catching up a battalion of Saxons, we advanced with them and crossed the Meuse by one of the pontoon bridges, which had been built that morning. Bazeilles, Balan, and Douzy were in front—Sedan farther ahead, perhaps four or five miles.

From a mountain on the right bank of the Meuse a German battery was grenading the three towns. Bazeilles was already in flames, The little station at the foot of the hills of Bazeilles was damaged by grenades; empty carriages were drawn up on the line by which Napoleon had escaped the previous day; and the whole country was covered with troops. Crossing the railway, I heard the rattle of the *mitrailleuses. R-r-r-r-r-r!* An infernal sound it is—like the death-rattle in a giant's throat. The noise is appalling. It *"takes the steam"* out of one.

Across the fields we marched in quick time. We were now in the battle. The Saxon battalion's band suddenly struck up the *"Sardanapalus March"*—the most glorious tune I ever stepped to. Its effect upon everybody was electrical. Those who had drooped under the weight of their arms, sprang up as "fresh" as they had been; there was no lagging now; but without a word the Saxons advanced, battalion after battalion, The roar of the cannons and the rattle of the rifles and *mitrailleuses* increased in intensity; grenades fell everywhere; shrapnel exploded our midst; the *sanitaats* men were carrying off the wounded; the town of Bazeilles in our rear was a mass of red flame and smoke.

Leaving the infantry, who halted for a while, my companion and I pressed on over the ploughed ground, listening intently, as we ran up the bill, for the premonitory whistle of the shrapnel, which, exploding high above us, were dealing out death all around. Encumbered with a heavy knapsack, a bag, and a rug, blinded by the sun, half-fainting from the heat, and fatigued with the long run, I had some difficulty in ascending the hills. I threw my bag away, and thus relieved of some of my *impedimenta*, I gained a small coppice on the slope of the hill, near the Château D'Orival. Here a battalion of infantry had taken shelter. But there was more danger in the woods than in the open fields.

The French threw grenades and shrapnel into the coppice, and bullets did their deadly work too well. Men were falling close to me. On the hill was a battery of six guns—No. 3 of the Fourth Army Corps—commanded by Captain Richter. The position of this battery (to which I was subsequently attached for nearly three months) was admirable. From the crest of the hill at Bazeilles, its guns swept the whole valley and the series of heights beyond, where the French had placed their batteries of cannon, and their *mitrailleuses*, which maintained a raking fire. The officers and men were chatting as unconcernedly as though it had been a review at Berlin, instead of the greatest battle of the war! Meanwhile a shower of leaden hail was falling, and decimating the ranks of both infantry and artillery. A few yards from where I stood watching the terrible fight between the infantry in the valley in front, a grenade exploded, and killed an artilleryman and two horses.

The scene at this time was one of awful grandeur. Batteries of German artillery were in position on each side of the two rivers, the Meuse and the Chiers. Brevilly, Pelaigue, Nouilly, and Waldincourt were also in possession of the Germans. The French occupied positions just beyond Bazeilles, and at the villages of Balan and Douzy, their right wing being close to Sedan, the guns of which fortress supported it. At Nouilly was the staff of the King's army. The French fought with the desperation of men who knew that they were playing their last card. Early in the day they lost their commander-in-chief, Marshal Mac-Mahon, who was badly wounded, and compelled to resign the command to General de Wimpffen, in whom the soldiers had little confidence.

Napoleon was in front of his army, and, sword in hand, encouraged them. The French were, however, outnumbered, and, as usual, out-generalled. Moltke's plan of battle was to surround the enemy, and this, by the aid of the Bavarians and Saxons, he succeeded in doing.

With the din of battle ringing in my ears, I descended into the outskirts of Bazeilles—then burning rapidly—to procure some water. I entered a *château* for this purpose, and had just revived myself by drinking a little water, scooped up in my hands, when, as I was about to repair to my original position, I was arrested by a Prussian soldier, who, holding his *zünt-nadel* before me, obstructed my progress. I showed, him my "*legitimation*," but he either could not or would not comprehend its meaning. He insisted on my remaining with him; but my duty was in the front, where alone I could witness what it was my business to describe. I ran towards an officer who was galloping past, hailed him, and produced my authority to go wherever I wished; and he directed the man to return to his post, I was watching the battle from another point, when an officer of the Fourth Army Corps, who was taking ammunition to the front—an advance by the Germans being now made—asked me if I would care to take a seat in one of the wagons. I willingly assented, and rode forward.

Our way was through fields covered with the dead and dying of both armies. Some were lying with their hands crossed on their breasts, their glassy eyes fixed upon the blue vault of Heaven; others lay, as they fell, in a heap; some had fallen into the ditches and streams that permeated the valley; a French *chasseur*, shot through the heart, was lying in a streamlet, his head resting on his knees, and his rifle still grasped firmly in both hands. A ghastly sight it was, and one that is printed indelibly on my memory. It was now noon, and the French were slowly retiring towards Sedan. Nothing could resist the onward movement of the German troops, who kept up a perpetual *enfilade*.

The second position occupied by the batteries of the Fourth

Army Corps was beyond Bazeilles. Here we were in much greater danger than before. There was no cessation of grenades and *chassepôt* bullets. They fell thickly around us, while many whistled harmlessly over our heads. On the *plateau*, near the batteries (which, by the way, were never silent), I saw in the afternoon General (now Count) von Moltke, General von Alvenslaben, General Schöler, General the Prince of Rudolstadt, and many other distinguished officers. The king and the crown prince were on the hills to the left, near the Meuse.

We remained in this position all the afternoon. By four o'clock the battle was virtually over. The *corps d'armée* of General Wimpffen, Lebrun, Ducrot, and Felix Douay were beaten; it was impossible to retreat upon Mezières, as had been intended; the *chasseurs* and the 2nd Chasseurs d'Afrique had rushed "*into the jaws of death*;" and then came a general rout. The Prussian cavalry were sent in pursuit, and before six. o'clock the white flag floating on the citadel of Sedan indicated the throwing-up of the sponge. The disaster to France was complete. I believe if I put the Prussian losses at 33,000 killed and wounded I shall not be exceeding the number; the French loss was at least 40,000 killed and wounded.

That night Napoleon proposed to surrender himself, his army of 80,000 men, and ammunition and war *matériel*; and the following morning witnessed the actual surrender. The terms of capitulation were arranged between Generals de Wimpffen and Moltke in cottage near Sedan; and that day (the 2nd of September) Napoleon was removed to Bellevue Castle, near Frenois, having given up his sword to the king in person.

On the night of the battle I bivouacked with the Saxons on the field, amongst dead and wounded, and in view of the three burning towns, Bazeilles, Willers-Cernay, and Waldincourt. At 10 p.m. we received an order to march back for three miles; we accordingly had two bivouacs in one night.

CHAPTER 16

After Sedan

After the Battle of Sedan[1] and the surrender of the emperor and his army, we all thought the worse was over, and there were mutual congratulations upon the termination of the campaign. On the morning of the 2nd of September the Saxon army received orders to be in readiness to march at any moment, but whether our destination was Paris or Prussia nobody knew. That night we bivouacked on the battlefield at Bazeilles. Before darkness set in a storm swept over the hills; the wind blew a gale, and rain fell in torrents. A few officers rejoiced in the possession of *tentes d'abri*, which they had captured from the French, but in our division there was not one tent of any kind.

At eight o'clock we turned-in, if that may be called "turning-in" when we were too plainly "turned-out." The cannon were drawn up in a row; the horses were picketed in the rear of the guns; fires blazed redly here and through the mist and smoke; on the slope of the hills were drawn up the wagons of the *markten-ters* and those of the *proviant*-column in front of as the battlefield was still dotted with the bodies of the dead; in the valley the houses at Bazeilles, and the sister villages, which were set on fire on the previous day, still burnt.

As we stretched ourselves on the wet ground, with nothing under us but Mother Earth, the rain fell faster than before, and

---

1. *Two Accounts of the Battle of Sedan, 1st September 1870, The Battle of Sedan* by George W. A. Fitz-George and *Battlefield of Sedan* by C. W. Robinson also published by Leonaur.

we were wet to the skin in a few minutes. With my knapsack for a pillow, I crouched under a cannon, curled myself up, and endeavoured to sleep. But the rain trickled down my back, the wind cut like a sword, the horses plunged about so furiously that the Seven Sleepers would have been awakened by the uproar. Grumbling—the Briton's usual privilege—was of no use whatever. Everybody was is the same predicament, with the exception of those few officers who had the *tentes d'abri* and those men who had endeavoured to protect themselves from the elements by erecting rough huts made of the boughs of trees.

With the first dawn of day we sprang up, made coffee in the rain, which had never ceased, and prepared, wet through as we were, to march. The parade was at six o'clock—we did not march until ten, when we slowly moved off the battlefield, some of us sick at heart as we thought of the thousands of brave men whose blood reddened the hills and fields. Leaving the Bavarians in bivouac near Bazeilles, we crossed the blue waters of the Meuse by the pontoon bridges which still remained, and made our first halt at Hauraucourt, about an hour's march from Bazeilles, having passed through fields and over roads knee-deep in mud, and littered with war debris of all descriptions.

At Hauraucourt—a delightful village—I happened to stumble into the house of a worthy miller who dwells by the side of a much smaller stream than the famed river Dee, and who, if not quite as "jolly" a personage as he whose praises are sung in the lyric, was largely possessed of the virtue of hospitality. His wife no sooner heard that I was in search of a bed and something to eat, than she proceeded to satisfy my wants, giving me the best chamber the house afforded, and setting before me *café au lait*, eggs, and good brown bread and butter, *Madame* was full of regrets that there should have been so much blood shed, and, with her husband, her daughter, and her mother—an aged dame who had lost all her teeth, but who was yet able to talk as volubly as her daughter— joined in unmitigated abuse of the emperor, and in a prayer for his speedy death by the guillotine! And this, by the way, was the universally-expressed opinion of the people in the provinces.

Passing the town of Raucourt, where the people were apparently settling down to their business again, we marched *via* Maisoncelles and Ghémery to Vendresse—now fairly *en route* to Paris. Arrived at Vendresse, we found there was no bread to be had, and nothing in the shops excepting a little coffee, a few bottles of wine, and half a dozen pounds of butchers' meat. The butcher was killing an ox as we entered the town; but what was one ox amongst so many men? I managed to purchase a small piece of mutton, and went off under the impression that I had made a good investment.

Nor was there reason to complain on the score of quantity. There was a pound and a half, or thereabouts, and it looked more. It was the quality that caused me to inveigh against that Vendresse butcher, whose meat was so tough that the united molars of seven Prussian soldiers were unavailing in their attempts to masticate it. The men became furious when they found that there was nothing to eat. Foraging parties were organized, and every house in the town and vicinity was visited in turn. Those peasants who vehemently denied having anything fit to eat or drink had to submit to an inspection of their cellars and cupboards, in both of which something was generally found, and, of course, confiscated. Any cow, sheep, or pig which happened to wandering in the streets or roads was the object of immediate attention. Nothing escaped the lynx-eyed soldiers. A fat porker striving to escape down a drain was prodded by a sabre, and dragged ignominiously into the road, where a fire was lit and the sacrifice offered.

We were early astir on the following morning Tuesday, September 6, and we left Vendresse before six o'clock had struck. There are few sights as picturesque as that of an army on the march. Of course the baggage of an army corps is considerable. By the word "baggage" is not meant personal luggage—for that is very limited in quantity, each officer being allowed only space for a email portmanteau—but the necessaries for an army comprising all branches of the service. These include, amongst other things, spare wheels for the artillery, gun-carriages, and waggons, hatchets and spades for the use of the pioneers, large quantities of ammunition, and everything required for the wounded—coffee, rice, bread, pork, and bacon (*speck*), *zwieback* (biscuit as hard as that eaten by seamen), and so many other articles that their enumeration would be difficult.

There are quite 200 baggage waggons attached to a Prussian army corps, and these, with their one, two, or three horses, and their white sailcloth coverings, form an imposing sight of themselves, stretching as they do for a couple of English miles. Then there are the carriages in which the members of the General Staff are conveyed from place to place, vehicles containing the baggage of the generals of divisions, others for the *feld-post* officials and the letters and newspapers which are dispatched and received all along the line of route. For the last-named carriages a most careful watch is kept by everybody, and the officials are treated with the utmost respect.

It must not be imagined that any of the vehicles mentioned are of the class one is accustomed to see in Rotten Row. On the contrary, these Prussian carriages are of a very "ramshackle" description—dirty (apparently they are never washed), ill-painted, uncomfortable *wagens*, such as would not sell in England for £20 each, take them one with another. They are, in fact, like most German carriages, exceedingly disreputable-looking, bearing a close affinity to those vehicles one sees in the neighbourhood of Piccadilly and the Haymarket between three and five o'clock in the morning, with a drunken "fare" insisting that the proper place for his feet is outside the cab window. Such, then, are these carriages of the Prussian army, which either precede or follow the column.

The General of Division, the Major-General, and the numerous officers composing the staff; the infantry, with their rifles at the shoulder; the pontoon waggons; the artillery, with its sturdy horsemen, and its guard of three men to each gun and waggon; the hussars, in their handsome blue uniform; the light cavalry, dragoons, *cuirassiers*, mounted officers of all grades, servants leading spare horses, mules laden with officers' baggage; and, perhaps, a carriage containing one or two newspaper correspondents, who are expected to be everywhere at once—this is the formation of an army corps on the march: and as the column defiled through one of those beautiful forest-glades so numerous in France, with the morning sun glistening upon the bayonets and swords and the burnished helmets, the scene was wonderfully picturesque.

The scenery of the Ardennes, near Montigny, is unequalled in the east of France; and the weather was fortunately fine enough to enable us to fully enjoy it. Undulating, park-like ground, with pollards and elms lining, the fields, and glorious coppices on each side, are succeeded by orchards which you never see the last of until you reach the vast plains around Soissons, It is a great cider-making district, answering to Devonshire, Herefordshire, and Somersetshire, and a ride through it at this season of the year is delightful. You pass a forest of orchards—apples are everywhere. They are of every description and colour, from the deep crimson-tinted fruit which in England are locally known as "Taunton beauties," down to the small yellow apple not much larger than a good-sized cherry.

For a whole week we marched through this apple-country, over which autumn was fast casting its many-hued mantle, and giving it that repose and colour which make the season so charming. The proprietors of the land allow not an inch to remain uncultivated. Between the apple-trees are grown potatoes and clover in large quantities; wheat, barley, beans, and mangold-wurzel being the other principal objects of cultivation in the district, in which are also pastures as rich as those the fairest English counties can show.

A noticeable feature of the district through which we marched was that every village has its church, no matter how small the place may be, or how near it is to other villages; and here they are so close that sometimes only an English mile separates them. The burial-grounds, sometimes attached to the church and sometimes situated at a little distance from it, after the fashion of our cemeteries at home, are as full of little crosses as graves. You see black and white crosses on the entrance-gates, and crucifixes on the tombstones, and at the entrance to every village is a tall crucifix, with the principal object rudely fashioned; and frequently decorated with a wreath of wheat or flowers.

The cross itself is of wood, with the figure carved in stone or some softer substance and occasionally an attempt at the construction of a plinth. These emblems are so numerous that the sacred character which should belong to them is lost by their constant repetition. Then is, however, a picturesqueness about them which one would not willingly miss.

En route to Villets-Cotterets, we passed the little town of Vielleront, which lies at the foot of a hill, hidden by trees from outward gaze. There are stone quarries here; masses of rough unhewn stone are scattered by the side of the road, which is darkened by the heavy foliage overhanging it; you can just see the houses and the railway station below by peeping through the trees; and when you reach the bridge crossing the iron way at a great height, such a scene bursts full upon the view as a painter would love to dwell upon while a poet would go into ecstasies at the nature-picture.

In a park a few yards from the road is the *château* of the Viscomte de la Montesquoieu—a large building of white stone. The *château* is flanked at both its eastern and its western end by the ruins of what was either an abbatial or a monastic edifice. At the western end of the *château* the ruined building is enshrouded by ivy, masses of which are pendent from its crumbling walls. Eastwards, the ruin takes a bolder shape, and there yet remains the orifice of what was once a rose window, probably of great beauty. Here a cluster of elms puts the house in shadow, and gives additional splendour to the *ensemble*. In the park before the *château* the waters of a pellucid stream reflect *château*, ruins, trees, and meadows, whilst the tall, sword-like grass which grows all around, and the forest that environs the domain, make the scene one of surpassing magnificence. It is a veritable bit of fairyland.

Between Villers-Cotterets and Plessis-Belleville the main

road, as is the case in other parts of the *arondissement*, is paved in the centre with huge stones. These, in many places, had been taken up, either by French soldiers or the peasants—of course with the intention of retarding, the progress of the enemy. This endeavour to impede the march of the Prussian army was, however, unavailing, for both sides of the highway being of soft earth and grass, along these the troops made their progress. We found Plessis-Belleville a deserted village as much as "sweet Auburn." I did not see half-a-dozen persons in the place. The shops, with a few worthless articles left in them, were deserted by their owners, regardless of consequences; private residences were closed, and the furniture and all that was valuable removed; the inhabitants had fled to Paris!

The artillery occupied the house of M. Rommetin, which forms one corner of a large quadrangle of farm buildings. The poultry and a couple of half-starved gray horses were all that the proprietor had left behind him; the former were speedily appropriated, whilst one of the latter fell a prey to the equine tastes of one of our most indefatigable camp-followers. In the house, nothing remained but the bed-furniture, a few chairs and tables, a little preserved fruit, some feminine finery, and the school books of *Mademoiselle*, who, I trust, found them intact on her return home, geographies, histories, books of devotion, and all. What few articles of clothing were useful, the *soldaten* appropriated, as a matter of course, but, altogether, they were not worth a £5 note.

We rested at Plessis-Belleville a whole day. From Plessis-Belleville the march on Sunday, September 18, was to Goussainville, a journey which occupied ten hours. *En route*, we passed Dammartin, where all the houses and all the shops, with the exception of the apothecaries' and the bakers', were closed, the few inhabitants who remained in the town congregating at their doors to see the corps march by. The *petite ville* of Villeneuve-sous-Dammartin was as quiet as though all the inhabitants were resting in the little churchyard instead of at Paris, whither they had fled a day or two before the arrival of the corps. The priest's servant was taking in his master's surplice as we passed the village, but if *M. le Curé* intended to say Mass that morning he must have performed that ceremony in an empty church, for the only people in the place were himself, his servant, and a faded female of the Gamp species, who was basking in the sunshine near a large chesnut tree.

At Roissy we encountered the second attempt to hinder us from proceeding. This was a barricade composed of large elm trees and huge paving stones, which extended for some fifty yards. Our pioneers, however, cleared the way, and in a few minutes we were marching through the town, which was as deserted as the other place we had passed, The corps rested at Roissy and Goussainville, at both of which places the houses had to be opened forcibly with hatchets and swords, their former occupiers having locked and bolted the doors.

Thus far we had seen nothing of the enemy, On the morning of the 19th of September, however, we were informed that a reconnoitring party had observed the French Mobile Guards in force at Pierrefitte, near Sarcelles. The Fourth Army Corps (General von Alvensleben's) was consequently drawn up in battle order on the bills near Goussainville, and, after waiting for two hours in expectation of an attack, moved on in the direction of Sarcelles. Every house in the town was empty. The window-blinds were drawn down, and the shops were barred and shuttered. Half-a-dozen men were all we saw in the place. Some regiments were sent on—others remained in the long street of Sarcelles.

The town is almost in a line with St. Denis, and immediately the French gunners saw our advance they began to throw grenades. The enemy were soon dislodged from the heights of Mont du Haut Roi, near Arnonville, of which they had taken possession, and driven out of small fort which was defended by *Turcos* and *Zouaves*. As we advanced to take up position, and as the artillery was going through an orchard, I saw lying by the wayside a drummer. One hand still grasped his tambour, but the drumsticks would never rattle again—they might have been in

Berlin for all the use they were to him; for the Angel of Death had laid his icy clutch upon the little drummer, and he had escaped Wörth, and Weissemburg, and Beaumont, and Sedan, to die of dysentery in sight of Paris.

There was no time to bury him, so there he lay, on a bank by the side of the road, his pale face looking up to Heaven, and his glassy eyes fixed on all who passed by. We waited in the street of Sarcelles for some time, anxiously awaiting information of what was going on in front, for there was incessant firing for more than an hour. The 2nd and 3rd batteries of artillery of the Eighth Division were drawn up by the side of the road; the infantry were sent forward; and in a few minutes the Prussian cavalry were scouring the country on all sides. At one o'clock we received the order to advance, and we did so, taking up position in a vineyard near the mountain referred to.

The Prussian infantry swarmed up the steep hillside, and opened a raking fire upon the French in front of St. Denis. The engagement lasted until four o'clock, and we were in reserve the whole time. This was all the more annoying, as several grenades came over the mountain and fell near us. Three exploded within a few yards of the spot where we were waiting. We heard the whistle and rush of the missiles as they flew towards us, and no one could say where they would fall. When they did come, however, not a man moved—not one soldier "ducked" his head to escape the probable effects of the grenades—all stood as calmly in their places as though they were listening to the melodies of Strauss or Offenbach instead of to the infernal music of the Fransozen cannon. The losses were very small in this engagement, the only important result of which was to let the enemy know the Prussians were in force outside Paris, and that the siege had begun.

After the engagement that day we rested Groslay, and on the following morning, instead of remaining before St. Denis to resume the battle, proceeded to Margency, a village close to Montmorency, through which charming town we also passed. Instead of houses with bed-furniture hanging from the windows, and streets of debris, we had a *vista* of handsome mansions, verdant lawns, the perfume of many flowers in place of the smell of powder, delightful *châteaux*, and well-kept roads, built of bright red brick, with white stone copings, and faced with the same material, situated on elevated ground in the midst of a very grove of greenery and flowers, with a background composed of a bank of firs, elms, oaks, and ash-trees.

These villas at Montmorency are ideal edifices. There are, besides, *châteaux*, constructed of warm-coloured wood, and entered by high ranges of stairs on each side, which are so picturesque that Messrs. Grieve and Telbin, and the other gentlemen who devote their time to stage decoration, should visit Montmorency immediately event! allow of their doing so, if only to sketch one charming *château* near the railway, which is a picture of itself. It was here that the Pompadour lived, and Louis Quatorze had no more pleasant resort than this same town of Montmorency. Margency and Andilly were the next abiding-places of the Fourth Army Corps.

From Andilly you have a magnificent view of Paris—the gilded dome of the Invalides, the Arc de Triomphe, the top of the Champs Elysées, and the Bois de Boulogne; the Madeleine is visible to the naked eye, and we could see the fortifications of the capital. Eastward is St. Denis. It was a splendid sight, the great city, its arch, churches, and countless houses, and our evenings at Andilly passed very pleasantly in the contemplation of the doomed town. From Montmorency we could see the soldiers on the ramparts at Montmartre, and hear the operatives at work in St. Denis.

CHAPTER 17

An Awkward Position

We bade farewell to Montmorency on the 16th of October, and took up our quarters at St. Gratien—a small town about four miles from Montmorency. We found St. Gratien and the neighbourhood full of "Lazareth," for fever was still rife in the Saxon army. Our first business was to secure comfortable quarters—not an easy matter when almost every house was occupied by infantry. Living in the charming villas of Montmorency had made us all fastidious, and we changed our quarters three times on the day of our arrival at St. Gratien, before we finally settled down in a large house in full view of the French forts. There being nothing to do after having secured our quarters, an artillery officer proposed a visit to Mont d'Orgemont, a proposition in which I concurred, for there was some likelihood of seeing what the enemy was about.

We left the town at noon, after our modest *déjeuner* of bread and wine, and in five minutes were wandering among the vineyards and orchards and vegetable gardens which intervene between St. Gratien and Mont d'Orgemont. Making our way through the vines upon which the purple fruits hung in rich clusters, we soon arrived at a position sufficiently elevated to enable us to see St. Denis, its churches, tall factory chimneys, the numerous batteries, and the Seine flowing placidly along in the calmness of the autumn morning. A little to the east of the town is a large *château* environed by trees, and as silent and desolate that morning as the houses of Montmorency and Andilly.

There are gardens and vineyards for many miles round; these were dotted by soldiers getting in the necessary vegetables for the day, and unregardful of their proximity to the Fransozen guns. With the red and white mansions of Montmorency making the most picturesque background, the *coup d'oeil* is charming, and on any other occasion would have caused us to linger admiringly; but this was not what we came out to see. Our motto was "*Excelsior*," and, bearing in mind the fate of the melancholy and youthful hero of the poem we clambered onward through the obstructive vines and the tall asparagus running rapidly *to* seed, and clinging to the feet in a manner which made walking next to impossible.

We had not gone a quarter of a mile ere we met two of the *verposten* returning to the town from their position on the top of the mountain. Inquiring of them the best position for observation, we were directs to a ruined house on the summit of Mont d'Orgemont. This, they said, was the place above all others from whence to see St. Denis and Paris; but they added, with a smile on their swarthy faces, "the grenades come thickly there."

"Oh," said my companion, "that is nothing;" and we ascended the mountain, striking now and then into the bridle-road. A few paces higher, and we adjusted our glasses, and had just got them focussed on St. Denis, when the unpleasant sound emitted by a grenade in its flight through the air saluted our ears. "*Prenez garde*," shouted my companion, but ere the words had escaped from his lips we were both lying flat on the ground, under an apple-tree—no sort of protection from a grenade, but the only cover of any description near at hand, and one's first thought in such an emergency is to seek some kind of shelter, no matter what.

We had not time to watch for the course which the missile was taking, for we could not see from whence it came, and you could barely have counted ten before the explosion came, the grenade was burying itself in the ground, and the dust was flying in the air. I don't know if any who read this have ever experienced the sensation produced by these aerial messengers of death. The blood rushes hotly through your veins, your, cheeks flush, your heart beats with inconceivable rapidity and loudness. It is a fearful moment, that occupied by the flight of the grenade towards you. "Ha, they see us from the fort below," said my friend, speaking German at a terrible pace. "They see us, and are firing in this direction."

This was a pleasant position for a correspondent! There was no cover to retire into, we were in full view of the enemy, and had about a half a mile to walk ere we came to the house to which I have referred. We walked slowly up the mountain side, for it avails nothing to hide away from a cannon-ball or a grenade, which is sure to find you out if it is intended for you in less than three minutes, as we were looking at the valley through which the Seine flows by the fort which was taking so great an interest in us, the second grenade came. It fell short by about twenty yards, but the line of trail was good, and it was tolerably evident that number three would be a better shot than its predecessors.

En attendant we took a glance at the level ground below, and discovered the source of the grenades. They were thrown from a small fort which the enemy had recently constructed during the night close to the Seine. It was isolated from the batteries of St. Denis and the fortifications of Paris, and stood in a large field by the river. We reached the summit of Mont d'Orgemont without being hit by the grenades. It was an extraordinary place. There are two houses on the summit—ruined buildings, for many grenades have been fired into them. One, at least was constructed for defensive purposes, for as yet remained the embrasures. A hundred yards below, sheltered by a wall, lay the ?Prussian? foreposts, one company of infantry. The men were lying about in the sun, with their arms piled, and the scene was extremely picturesque.

Of course the Republicans knew that the house was occupied by the foreposts, and, equally of course, they sent their grenades as near as they could to the little band. As we were looking down upon the foreposts, a third grenade was thrown, and we took shelter behind the ruined house.

In the rear of the building there is an immense quarry of stone and sandstone, as well as two small houses, once used as dwellings, but now having the roofs forced in and the rafters charred by the French grenades. The ground, surrounding the quarry, being very high, offers, excellent opportunities for looking out, and we clambered up its wet clayey sides until we were so close to the Arc de Triomphe that the Champs Elysées were plainly visible. In St. Denis we saw a locomotive with a few carriages attached to it, the first train we had seen for more than two months.

We were in too good a position to escape the notice of the vigilant gunners of the Seine, who despatched a fourth grenade after us immediately on our presence being observed. From this time, for an hour, we were not free from these unwelcome guests, which found us out, go wherever we would. They fell so thickly in front at last that we were fain obliged to retreat down the side of the mountain, my companion by one route and I by another, and both across country. The grenades followed us for more than a mile and a half, and it was only by halting directly we heard the report and watching their flight that we escaped. Each of us thought the other had been struck by the missiles, and our meeting in the street leading to the town was, I need hardly say, marked by the warmest mutual congratulations.

Concerning the siege of Paris, I had and have no intention of entering into details. So great an event in military history demands a separate chronicle. An abler pen than mine will doubtless place on permanent record the varied incidents of the siege, which terminates as I add these concluding words. Before writing *Finis*, however, I would be ungrateful and ungracious not to acknowledge the many kindnesses and assistance which I received from my Prussian, Bavarian, and Saxon friends, and more especially from the members of the general staff of General von Schöler's division and the officers and men of Captain Richter's artillery battery.

ALSO FROM LEONAUR
AVAILABLE IN SOFTCOVER OR HARDCOVER WITH DUST JACKET

AT THEM WITH THE BAYONET by *Donald F. Featherstone*—The first Anglo-Sikh War 1845-1846.

STEPHEN CRANE'S BATTLES by *Stephen Crane*—Nine Decisive Battles Recounted by the Author of 'The Red Badge of Courage'.

THE GURKHA WAR by *H. T. Prinsep*—The Anglo-Nepalese Conflict in North East India 1814-1816.

FIRE & BLOOD by *G. R. Gleig*—The burning of Washington & the battle of New Orleans, 1814, through the eyes of a young British soldier.

SOUND ADVANCE! by *Joseph Anderson*—Experiences of an officer of HM 50th regiment in Australia, Burma & the Gwalior war.

THE CAMPAIGN OF THE INDUS by *Thomas Holdsworth*—Experiences of a British Officer of the 2nd (Queen's Royal) Regiment in the Campaign to Place Shah Shuja on the Throne of Afghanistan 1838 - 1840.

WITH THE MADRAS EUROPEAN REGIMENT IN BURMA by *John Butler*—The Experiences of an Officer of the Honourable East India Company's Army During the First Anglo-Burmese War 1824 - 1826.

IN ZULULAND WITH THE BRITISH ARMY by *Charles L. Norris-Newman*—The Anglo-Zulu war of 1879 through the first-hand experiences of a special correspondent.

BESIEGED IN LUCKNOW by *Martin Richard Gubbins*—The first Anglo-Sikh War 1845-1846.

A TIGER ON HORSEBACK by *L. March Phillips*—The Experiences of a Trooper & Officer of Rimington's Guides - The Tigers - during the Anglo-Boer war 1899 - 1902.

SEPOYS, SIEGE & STORM by *Charles John Griffiths*—The Experiences of a young officer of H.M.'s 61st Regiment at Ferozepore, Delhi ridge and at the fall of Delhi during the Indian mutiny 1857.

CAMPAIGNING IN ZULULAND by *W. E. Montague*—Experiences on campaign during the Zulu war of 1879 with the 94th Regiment.

THE STORY OF THE GUIDES by *G.J. Younghusband*—The Exploits of the Soldiers of the famous Indian Army Regiment from the northwest frontier 1847 - 1900.

AVAILABLE ONLINE AT **www.leonaur.com**
AND FROM ALL GOOD BOOK STORES

ALSO FROM LEONAUR
AVAILABLE IN SOFTCOVER OR HARDCOVER WITH DUST JACKET

ZULU:1879 by D.C.F. Moodie & the Leonaur Editors—The Anglo-Zulu War of 1879 from contemporary sources: First Hand Accounts, Interviews, Dispatches, Official Documents & Newspaper Reports.

THE RED DRAGOON by W.J. Adams—With the 7th Dragoon Guards in the Cape of Good Hope against the Boers & the Kaffir tribes during the 'war of the axe' 1843-48'.

THE RECOLLECTIONS OF SKINNER OF SKINNER'S HORSE by James Skinner—James Skinner and his 'Yellow Boys' Irregular cavalry in the wars of India between the British, Mahratta, Rajput, Mogul, Sikh & Pindarree Forces.

A CAVALRY OFFICER DURING THE SEPOY REVOLT by A. R. D. Mackenzie—Experiences with the 3rd Bengal Light Cavalry, the Guides and Sikh Irregular Cavalry from the outbreak to Delhi and Lucknow.

A NORFOLK SOLDIER IN THE FIRST SIKH WAR by J W Baldwin—Experiences of a private of H.M. 9th Regiment of Foot in the battles for the Punjab, India 1845-6.

TOMMY ATKINS' WAR STORIES: 14 FIRST HAND ACCOUNTS—Fourteen first hand accounts from the ranks of the British Army during Queen Victoria's Empire.

THE WATERLOO LETTERS by H. T. Siborne—Accounts of the Battle by British Officers for its Foremost Historian.

NEY: GENERAL OF CAVALRY VOLUME 1—1769-1799 by Antoine Bulos—The Early Career of a Marshal of the First Empire.

NEY: MARSHAL OF FRANCE VOLUME 2—1799-1805 by Antoine Bulos—The Early Career of a Marshal of the First Empire.

AIDE-DE-CAMP TO NAPOLEON by Philippe-Paul de Ségur—For anyone interested in the Napoleonic Wars this book, written by one who was intimate with the strategies and machinations of the Emperor, will be essential reading.

TWILIGHT OF EMPIRE by Sir Thomas Ussher & Sir George Cockburn—Two accounts of Napoleon's Journeys in Exile to Elba and St. Helena: Narrative of Events by Sir Thomas Ussher & Napoleon's Last Voyage: Extract of a diary by Sir George Cockburn.

PRIVATE WHEELER by William Wheeler—The letters of a soldier of the 51st Light Infantry during the Peninsular War & at Waterloo.

AVAILABLE ONLINE AT **www.leonaur.com**
AND FROM ALL GOOD BOOK STORES

ALSO FROM LEONAUR
AVAILABLE IN SOFTCOVER OR HARDCOVER WITH DUST JACKET

OFFICERS & GENTLEMEN *by Peter Hawker & William Graham*—Two Accounts of British Officers During the Peninsula War: Officer of Light Dragoons by Peter Hawker & Campaign in Portugal and Spain by William Graham .

THE WALCHEREN EXPEDITION *by Anonymous*—The Experiences of a British Officer of the 81st Regt. During the Campaign in the Low Countries of 1809.

LADIES OF WATERLOO *by Charlotte A. Eaton, Magdalene de Lancey & Juana Smith*—The Experiences of Three Women During the Campaign of 1815: Waterloo Days by Charlotte A. Eaton, A Week at Waterloo by Magdalene de Lancey & Juana's Story by Juana Smith.

JOURNAL OF AN OFFICER IN THE KING'S GERMAN LEGION *by John Frederick Hering*—Recollections of Campaigning During the Napoleonic Wars.

JOURNAL OF AN ARMY SURGEON IN THE PENINSULAR WAR *by Charles Boutflower*—The Recollections of a British Army Medical Man on Campaign During the Napoleonic Wars.

ON CAMPAIGN WITH MOORE AND WELLINGTON *by Anthony Hamilton*—The Experiences of a Soldier of the 43rd Regiment During the Peninsular War.

THE ROAD TO AUSTERLITZ *by R. G. Burton*—Napoleon's Campaign of 1805.

SOLDIERS OF NAPOLEON *by A. J. Doisy De Villargennes & Arthur Chuquet*—The Experiences of the Men of the French First Empire: Under the Eagles by A. J. Doisy De Villargennes & Voices of 1812 by Arthur Chuquet .

INVASION OF FRANCE, 1814 *by F. W. O. Maycock*—The Final Battles of the Napoleonic First Empire.

LEIPZIG—A CONFLICT OF TITANS *by Frederic Shoberl*—A Personal Experience of the 'Battle of the Nations' During the Napoleonic Wars, October 14th-19th, 1813.

SLASHERS *by Charles Cadell*—The Campaigns of the 28th Regiment of Foot During the Napoleonic Wars by a Serving Officer.

BATTLE IMPERIAL *by Charles William Vane*—The Campaigns in Germany & France for the Defeat of Napoleon 1813-1814.

SWIFT & BOLD *by Gibbes Rigaud*—The 60th Rifles During the Peninsula War.

AVAILABLE ONLINE AT **www.leonaur.com**
AND FROM ALL GOOD BOOK STORES

ALSO FROM LEONAUR
AVAILABLE IN SOFTCOVER OR HARDCOVER WITH DUST JACKET

ADVENTURES OF A YOUNG RIFLEMAN by Johann Christian Maempel—The Experiences of a Saxon in the French & British Armies During the Napoleonic Wars.

THE HUSSAR by Norbert Landsheit & G. R. Gleig—A German Cavalryman in British Service Throughout the Napoleonic Wars.

RECOLLECTIONS OF THE PENINSULA by Moyle Sherer—An Officer of the 34th Regiment of Foot—'The Cumberland Gentlemen'—on Campaign Against Napoleon's French Army in Spain.

MARINE OF REVOLUTION & CONSULATE by Moreau de Jonnès—The Recollections of a French Soldier of the Revolutionary Wars 1791-1804.

GENTLEMEN IN RED by John Dobbs & Robert Knowles—Two Accounts of British Infantry Officers During the Peninsular War Recollections of an Old 52nd Man by John Dobbs An Officer of Fusiliers by Robert Knowles.

CORPORAL BROWN'S CAMPAIGNS IN THE LOW COUNTRIES by Robert Brown—Recollections of a Coldstream Guard in the Early Campaigns Against Revolutionary France 1793-1795.

THE 7TH (QUEENS OWN) HUSSARS: Volume 2—1793-1815 by C. R. B. Barrett—During the Campaigns in the Low Countries & the Peninsula and Waterloo Campaigns of the Napoleonic Wars. Volume 2: 1793-1815.

THE MARENGO CAMPAIGN 1800 by Herbert H. Sargent—The Victory that Completed the Austrian Defeat in Italy.

DONALDSON OF THE 94TH—SCOTS BRIGADE by Joseph Donaldson—The Recollections of a Soldier During the Peninsula & South of France Campaigns of the Napoleonic Wars.

A CONSCRIPT FOR EMPIRE by Philippe as told to Johann Christian Maempel—The Experiences of a Young German Conscript During the Napoleonic Wars.

JOURNAL OF THE CAMPAIGN OF 1815 by Alexander Cavalié Mercer—The Experiences of an Officer of the Royal Horse Artillery During the Waterloo Campaign.

NAPOLEON'S CAMPAIGNS IN POLAND 1806-7 by Robert Wilson—The campaign in Poland from the Russian side of the conflict.

AVAILABLE ONLINE AT **www.leonaur.com**
AND FROM ALL GOOD BOOK STORES

ALSO FROM LEONAUR
AVAILABLE IN SOFTCOVER OR HARDCOVER WITH DUST JACKET

OMPTEDA OF THE KING'S GERMAN LEGION by *Christian von Ompteda*—A Hanoverian Officer on Campaign Against Napoleon.

LIEUTENANT SIMMONS OF THE 95TH (RIFLES) by *George Simmons*—Recollections of the Peninsula, South of France & Waterloo Campaigns of the Napoleonic Wars.

A HORSEMAN FOR THE EMPEROR by *Jean Baptiste Gazzola*—A Cavalryman of Napoleon's Army on Campaign Throughout the Napoleonic Wars.

SERGEANT LAWRENCE by *William Lawrence*—With the 40th Regt. of Foot in South America, the Peninsular War & at Waterloo.

CAMPAIGNS WITH THE FIELD TRAIN by *Richard D. Henegan*—Experiences of a British Officer During the Peninsula and Waterloo Campaigns of the Napoleonic Wars.

CAVALRY SURGEON by *S. D. Broughton*—On Campaign Against Napoleon in the Peninsula & South of France During the Napoleonic Wars 1812-1814.

MEN OF THE RIFLES by *Thomas Knight, Henry Curling & Jonathan Leach*—The Reminiscences of Thomas Knight of the 95th (Rifles) by Thomas Knight, Henry Curling's Anecdotes by Henry Curling & The Field Services of the Rifle Brigade from its Formation to Waterloo by Jonathan Leach.

THE ULM CAMPAIGN 1805 by *F. N. Maude*—Napoleon and the Defeat of the Austrian Army During the 'War of the Third Coalition'.

SOLDIERING WITH THE 'DIVISION' by *Thomas Garrety*—The Military Experiences of an Infantryman of the 43rd Regiment During the Napoleonic Wars.

SERGEANT MORRIS OF THE 73RD FOOT by *Thomas Morris*—The Experiences of a British Infantryman During the Napoleonic Wars-Including Campaigns in Germany and at Waterloo.

A VOICE FROM WATERLOO by *Edward Cotton*—The Personal Experiences of a British Cavalryman Who Became a Battlefield Guide and Authority on the Campaign of 1815.

NAPOLEON AND HIS MARSHALS by *J. T. Headley*—The Men of the First Empire.

AVAILABLE ONLINE AT **www.leonaur.com**
AND FROM ALL GOOD BOOK STORES

ALSO FROM LEONAUR
AVAILABLE IN SOFTCOVER OR HARDCOVER WITH DUST JACKET

COLBORNE: A SINGULAR TALENT FOR WAR by *John Colborne*—The Napoleonic Wars Career of One of Wellington's Most Highly Valued Officers in Egypt, Holland, Italy, the Peninsula and at Waterloo.

NAPOLEON'S RUSSIAN CAMPAIGN by *Philippe Henri de Segur*—The Invasion, Battles and Retreat by an Aide-de-Camp on the Emperor's Staff.

WITH THE LIGHT DIVISION by *John H. Cooke*—The Experiences of an Officer of the 43rd Light Infantry in the Peninsula and South of France During the Napoleonic Wars.

WELLINGTON AND THE PYRENEES CAMPAIGN VOLUME I: FROM VITORIA TO THE BIDASSOA by *F. C. Beatson*—The final phase of the campaign in the Iberian Peninsula.

WELLINGTON AND THE INVASION OF FRANCE VOLUME II: THE BIDASSOA TO THE BATTLE OF THE NIVELLE by *F. C. Beatson*—The final phase of the campaign in the Iberian Peninsula.

WELLINGTON AND THE FALL OF FRANCE VOLUME III: THE GAVES AND THE BATTLE OF ORTHEZ by *F. C. Beatson*—The final phase of the campaign in the Iberian Peninsula.

NAPOLEON'S IMPERIAL GUARD: FROM MARENGO TO WATERLOO by *J. T. Headley*—The story of Napoleon's Imperial Guard and the men who commanded them.

BATTLES & SIEGES OF THE PENINSULAR WAR by *W. H. Fitchett*—Corunna, Busaco, Albuera, Ciudad Rodrigo, Badajos, Salamanca, San Sebastian & Others.

SERGEANT GUILLEMARD: THE MAN WHO SHOT NELSON? by *Robert Guillemard*—A Soldier of the Infantry of the French Army of Napoleon on Campaign Throughout Europe.

WITH THE GUARDS ACROSS THE PYRENEES by *Robert Batty*—The Experiences of a British Officer of Wellington's Army During the Battles for the Fall of Napoleonic France, 1813 .

A STAFF OFFICER IN THE PENINSULA by *E. W. Buckham*—An Officer of the British Staff Corps Cavalry During the Peninsula Campaign of the Napoleonic Wars.

THE LEIPZIG CAMPAIGN: 1813—NAPOLEON AND THE "BATTLE OF THE NATIONS" by *F. N. Maude*—Colonel Maude's analysis of Napoleon's campaign of 1813 around Leipzig.

AVAILABLE ONLINE AT **www.leonaur.com**
AND FROM ALL GOOD BOOK STORES

ALSO FROM LEONAUR
AVAILABLE IN SOFTCOVER OR HARDCOVER WITH DUST JACKET

BUGEAUD: A PACK WITH A BATON *by Thomas Robert Bugeaud*—The Early Campaigns of a Soldier of Napoleon's Army Who Would Become a Marshal of France.

WATERLOO RECOLLECTIONS *by Frederick Llewellyn*—Rare First Hand Accounts, Letters, Reports and Retellings from the Campaign of 1815.

SERGEANT NICOL *by Daniel Nicol*—The Experiences of a Gordon Highlander During the Napoleonic Wars in Egypt, the Peninsula and France.

THE JENA CAMPAIGN: 1806 *by F. N. Maude*—The Twin Battles of Jena & Auerstadt Between Napoleon's French and the Prussian Army.

PRIVATE O'NEIL *by Charles O'Neil*—The recollections of an Irish Rogue of H. M. 28th Regt.—The Slashers—during the Peninsula & Waterloo campaigns of the Napoleonic war.

ROYAL HIGHLANDER *by James Anton*—A soldier of H.M 42nd (Royal) Highlanders during the Peninsular, South of France & Waterloo Campaigns of the Napoleonic Wars.

CAPTAIN BLAZE *by Elzéar Blaze*—Life in Napoleons Army.

LEJEUNE VOLUME 1 *by Louis-François Lejeune*—The Napoleonic Wars through the Experiences of an Officer on Berthier's Staff.

LEJEUNE VOLUME 2 *by Louis-François Lejeune*—The Napoleonic Wars through the Experiences of an Officer on Berthier's Staff.

CAPTAIN COIGNET *by Jean-Roch Coignet*—A Soldier of Napoleon's Imperial Guard from the Italian Campaign to Russia and Waterloo.

FUSILIER COOPER *by John S. Cooper*—Experiences in the 7th (Royal) Fusiliers During the Peninsular Campaign of the Napoleonic Wars and the American Campaign to New Orleans.

FIGHTING NAPOLEON'S EMPIRE *by Joseph Anderson*—The Campaigns of a British Infantryman in Italy, Egypt, the Peninsular & the West Indies During the Napoleonic Wars.

CHASSEUR BARRES *by Jean-Baptiste Barres*—The experiences of a French Infantryman of the Imperial Guard at Austerlitz, Jena, Eylau, Friedland, in the Peninsular, Lutzen, Bautzen, Zinnwald and Hanau during the Napoleonic Wars.

AVAILABLE ONLINE AT **www.leonaur.com**
AND FROM ALL GOOD BOOK STORES

ALSO FROM LEONAUR
AVAILABLE IN SOFTCOVER OR HARDCOVER WITH DUST JACKET

CAPTAIN COIGNET *by Jean-Roch Coignet*—A Soldier of Napoleon's Imperial Guard from the Italian Campaign to Russia and Waterloo.

HUSSAR ROCCA *by Albert Jean Michel de Rocca*—A French cavalry officer's experiences of the Napoleonic Wars and his views on the Peninsular Campaigns against the Spanish, British And Guerila Armies.

MARINES TO 95TH (RIFLES) *by Thomas Fernyhough*—The military experiences of Robert Fernyhough during the Napoleonic Wars.

LIGHT BOB *by Robert Blakeney*—The experiences of a young officer in H.M 28th & 36th regiments of the British Infantry during the Peninsular Campaign of the Napoleonic Wars 1804 - 1814.

WITH WELLINGTON'S LIGHT CAVALRY *by William Tomkinson*—The Experiences of an officer of the 16th Light Dragoons in the Peninsular and Waterloo campaigns of the Napoleonic Wars.

SERGEANT BOURGOGNE *by Adrien Bourgogne*—With Napoleon's Imperial Guard in the Russian Campaign and on the Retreat from Moscow 1812 - 13.

SURTEES OF THE 95TH (RIFLES) *by William Surtees*—A Soldier of the 95th (Rifles) in the Peninsular campaign of the Napoleonic Wars.

SWORDS OF HONOUR *by Henry Newbolt & Stanley L. Wood*—The Careers of Six Outstanding Officers from the Napoleonic Wars, the Wars for India and the American Civil War.

ENSIGN BELL IN THE PENINSULAR WAR *by George Bell*—The Experiences of a young British Soldier of the 34th Regiment 'The Cumberland Gentlemen' in the Napoleonic wars.

HUSSAR IN WINTER *by Alexander Gordon*—A British Cavalry Officer during the retreat to Corunna in the Peninsular campaign of the Napoleonic Wars.

THE COMPLEAT RIFLEMAN HARRIS *by Benjamin Harris as told to and transcribed by Captain Henry Curling, 52nd Regt. of Foot*—The adventures of a soldier of the 95th (Rifles) during the Peninsular Campaign of the Napoleonic Wars.

THE ADVENTURES OF A LIGHT DRAGOON *by George Farmer & G.R. Gleig*—A cavalryman during the Peninsular & Waterloo Campaigns, in captivity & at the siege of Bhurtpore, India.

AVAILABLE ONLINE AT **www.leonaur.com**
AND FROM ALL GOOD BOOK STORES

ALSO FROM LEONAUR
AVAILABLE IN SOFTCOVER OR HARDCOVER WITH DUST JACKET

THE LIFE OF THE REAL BRIGADIER GERARD VOLUME 1—THE YOUNG HUSSAR 1782-1807 *by Jean-Baptiste De Marbot*—A French Cavalryman Of the Napoleonic Wars at Marengo, Austerlitz, Jena, Eylau & Friedland.

THE LIFE OF THE REAL BRIGADIER GERARD VOLUME 2—IMPERIAL AIDE-DE-CAMP 1807-1811 *by Jean-Baptiste De Marbot*—A French Cavalryman of the Napoleonic Wars at Saragossa, Landshut, Eckmuhl, Ratisbon, Aspern-Essling, Wagram, Busaco & Torres Vedras.

THE LIFE OF THE REAL BRIGADIER GERARD VOLUME 3—COLONEL OF CHASSEURS 1811-1815 *by Jean-Baptiste De Marbot*—A French Cavalryman in the retreat from Moscow, Lutzen, Bautzen, Katzbach, Leipzig, Hanau & Waterloo.

THE INDIAN WAR OF 1864 *by Eugene Ware*—The Experiences of a Young Officer of the 7th Iowa Cavalry on the Western Frontier During the Civil War.

THE MARCH OF DESTINY *by Charles E. Young & V. Devinny*—Dangers of the Trail in 1865 by Charles E. Young & The Story of a Pioneer by V. Devinny, two Accounts of Early Emigrants to Colorado.

CROSSING THE PLAINS *by William Audley Maxwell*—A First Hand Narrative of the Early Pioneer Trail to California in 1857.

CHIEF OF SCOUTS *by William F. Drannan*—A Pilot to Emigrant and Government Trains, Across the Plains of the Western Frontier.

THIRTY-ONE YEARS ON THE PLAINS AND IN THE MOUNTAINS *by William F. Drannan*—William Drannan was born to be a pioneer, hunter, trapper and wagon train guide during the momentous days of the Great American West.

THE INDIAN WARS VOLUNTEER *by William Thompson*—Recollections of the Conflict Against the Snakes, Shoshone, Bannocks, Modocs and Other Native Tribes of the American North West.

THE 4TH TENNESSEE CAVALRY *by George B. Guild*—The Services of Smith's Regiment of Confederate Cavalry by One of its Officers.

COLONEL WORTHINGTON'S SHILOH *by T. Worthington*—The Tennessee Campaign, 1862, by an Officer of the Ohio Volunteers.

FOUR YEARS IN THE SADDLE *by W. L. Curry*—The History of the First Regiment Ohio Volunteer Cavalry in the American Civil War.

AVAILABLE ONLINE AT **www.leonaur.com**
AND FROM ALL GOOD BOOK STORES

ALSO FROM LEONAUR
AVAILABLE IN SOFTCOVER OR HARDCOVER WITH DUST JACKET

LIFE IN THE ARMY OF NORTHERN VIRGINIA by *Carlton McCarthy*—The Observations of a Confederate Artilleryman of Cutshaw's Battalion During the American Civil War 1861-1865.

HISTORY OF THE CAVALRY OF THE ARMY OF THE POTOMAC by *Charles D. Rhodes*—Including Pope's Army of Virginia and the Cavalry Operations in West Virginia During the American Civil War.

CAMP-FIRE AND COTTON-FIELD by *Thomas W. Knox*—A New York Herald Correspondent's View of the American Civil War.

SERGEANT STILLWELL by *Leander Stillwell*—The Experiences of a Union Army Soldier of the 61st Illinois Infantry During the American Civil War.

STONEWALL'S CANNONEER by *Edward A. Moore*—Experiences with the Rockbridge Artillery, Confederate Army of Northern Virginia, During the American Civil War.

THE SIXTH CORPS by *George Stevens*—The Army of the Potomac, Union Army, During the American Civil War.

THE RAILROAD RAIDERS by *William Pittenger*—An Ohio Volunteers Recollections of the Andrews Raid to Disrupt the Confederate Railroad in Georgia During the American Civil War.

CITIZEN SOLDIER by *John Beatty*—An Account of the American Civil War by a Union Infantry Officer of Ohio Volunteers Who Became a Brigadier General.

COX: PERSONAL RECOLLECTIONS OF THE CIVIL WAR--VOLUME 1 by *Jacob Dolson Cox*—West Virginia, Kanawha Valley, Gauley Bridge, Cotton Mountain, South Mountain, Antietam, the Morgan Raid & the East Tennessee Campaign.

COX: PERSONAL RECOLLECTIONS OF THE CIVIL WAR--VOLUME 2 by *Jacob Dolson Cox*—Siege of Knoxville, East Tennessee, Atlanta Campaign, the Nashville Campaign & the North Carolina Campaign.

KERSHAW'S BRIGADE VOLUME 1 by *D. Augustus Dickert*—Manassas, Seven Pines, Sharpsburg (Antietam), Fredricksburg, Chancellorsville, Gettysburg, Chickamauga, Chattanooga, Fort Sanders & Bean Station.

KERSHAW'S BRIGADE VOLUME 2 by *D. Augustus Dickert*—At the wilderness, Cold Harbour, Petersburg, The Shenandoah Valley and Cedar Creek..

AVAILABLE ONLINE AT **www.leonaur.com**
AND FROM ALL GOOD BOOK STORES

ALSO FROM LEONAUR
AVAILABLE IN SOFTCOVER OR HARDCOVER WITH DUST JACKET

THE RELUCTANT REBEL by *William G. Stevenson*—A young Kentuckian's experiences in the Confederate Infantry & Cavalry during the American Civil War..

BOOTS AND SADDLES by *Elizabeth B. Custer*—The experiences of General Custer's Wife on the Western Plains.

FANNIE BEERS' CIVIL WAR by *Fannie A. Beers*—A Confederate Lady's Experiences of Nursing During the Campaigns & Battles of the American Civil War.

LADY SALE'S AFGHANISTAN by *Florentia Sale*—An Indomitable Victorian Lady's Account of the Retreat from Kabul During the First Afghan War.

THE TWO WARS OF MRS DUBERLY by *Frances Isabella Duberly*—An Intrepid Victorian Lady's Experience of the Crimea and Indian Mutiny.

THE REBELLIOUS DUCHESS by *Paul F. S. Dermoncourt*—The Adventures of the Duchess of Berri and Her Attempt to Overthrow French Monarchy.

LADIES OF WATERLOO by *Charlotte A. Eaton, Magdalene de Lancey & Juana Smith*—The Experiences of Three Women During the Campaign of 1815: Waterloo Days by Charlotte A. Eaton, A Week at Waterloo by Magdalene de Lancey & Juana's Story by Juana Smith.

TWO YEARS BEFORE THE MAST by *Richard Henry Dana. Jr.*—The account of one young man's experiences serving on board a sailing brig—the Penelope—bound for California, between the years 1834-36.

A SAILOR OF KING GEORGE by *Frederick Hoffman*—From Midshipman to Captain—Recollections of War at Sea in the Napoleonic Age 1793-1815.

LORDS OF THE SEA by *A. T. Mahan*—Great Captains of the Royal Navy During the Age of Sail.

COGGESHALL'S VOYAGES: VOLUME 1 by *George Coggeshall*—The Recollections of an American Schooner Captain.

COGGESHALL'S VOYAGES: VOLUME 2 by *George Coggeshall*—The Recollections of an American Schooner Captain.

TWILIGHT OF EMPIRE by *Sir Thomas Ussher & Sir George Cockburn*—Two accounts of Napoleon's Journeys in Exile to Elba and St. Helena: Narrative of Events by Sir Thomas Ussher & Napoleon's Last Voyage: Extract of a diary by Sir George Cockburn.

AVAILABLE ONLINE AT **www.leonaur.com**
AND FROM ALL GOOD BOOK STORES

ALSO FROM LEONAUR
AVAILABLE IN SOFTCOVER OR HARDCOVER WITH DUST JACKET

ESCAPE FROM THE FRENCH by Edward Boys—A Young Royal Navy Midshipman's Adventures During the Napoleonic War.

THE VOYAGE OF H.M.S. PANDORA by Edward Edwards R. N. & George Hamilton, edited by Basil Thomson—In Pursuit of the Mutineers of the Bounty in the South Seas—1790-1791.

MEDUSA by J. B. Henry Savigny and Alexander Correard and Charlotte-Adélaïde Dard —Narrative of a Voyage to Senegal in 1816 & The Sufferings of the Picard Family After the Shipwreck of the Medusa.

THE SEA WAR OF 1812 VOLUME 1 by A. T. Mahan—A History of the Maritime Conflict.

THE SEA WAR OF 1812 VOLUME 2 by A. T. Mahan—A History of the Maritime Conflict.

WETHERELL OF H. M. S. HUSSAR by John Wetherell—The Recollections of an Ordinary Seaman of the Royal Navy During the Napoleonic Wars.

THE NAVAL BRIGADE IN NATAL by C. R. N. Burne—With the Guns of H. M. S. Terrible & H. M. S. Tartar during the Boer War 1899-1900.

THE VOYAGE OF H. M. S. BOUNTY by William Bligh—The True Story of an 18th Century Voyage of Exploration and Mutiny.

SHIPWRECK! by William Gilly—The Royal Navy's Disasters at Sea 1793-1849.

KING'S CUTTERS AND SMUGGLERS: 1700-1855 by E. Keble Chatterton—A unique period of maritime history-from the beginning of the eighteenth to the middle of the nineteenth century when British seamen risked all to smuggle valuable goods from wool to tea and spirits from and to the Continent.

CONFEDERATE BLOCKADE RUNNER by John Wilkinson—The Personal Recollections of an Officer of the Confederate Navy.

NAVAL BATTLES OF THE NAPOLEONIC WARS by W. H. Fitchett—Cape St. Vincent, the Nile, Cadiz, Copenhagen, Trafalgar & Others.

PRISONERS OF THE RED DESERT by R. S. Gwatkin-Williams—The Adventures of the Crew of the Tara During the First World War.

U-BOAT WAR 1914-1918 by James B. Connolly/Karl von Schenk—Two Contrasting Accounts from Both Sides of the Conflict at Sea D uring the Great War.

AVAILABLE ONLINE AT **www.leonaur.com**
AND FROM ALL GOOD BOOK STORES

ALSO FROM LEONAUR
AVAILABLE IN SOFTCOVER OR HARDCOVER WITH DUST JACKET

IRON TIMES WITH THE GUARDS *by An O. E. (G. P. A. Fildes)*—The Experiences of an Officer of the Coldstream Guards on the Western Front During the First World War.

THE GREAT WAR IN THE MIDDLE EAST: 1 *by W. T. Massey*—The Desert Campaigns & How Jerusalem Was Won---two classic accounts in one volume.

THE GREAT WAR IN THE MIDDLE EAST: 2 *by W. T. Massey*—Allenby's Final Triumph.

SMITH-DORRIEN *by Horace Smith-Dorrien*—Isandlwhana to the Great War.

1914 *by Sir John French*—The Early Campaigns of the Great War by the British Commander.

GRENADIER *by E. R. M. Fryer*—The Recollections of an Officer of the Grenadier Guards throughout the Great War on the Western Front.

BATTLE, CAPTURE & ESCAPE *by George Pearson*—The Experiences of a Canadian Light Infantryman During the Great War.

DIGGERS AT WAR *by R. Hugh Knyvett & G. P. Cuttriss*—"Over There" With the Australians by R. Hugh Knyvett and Over the Top With the Third Australian Division by G. P. Cuttriss. Accounts of Australians During the Great War in the Middle East, at Gallipoli and on the Western Front.

HEAVY FIGHTING BEFORE US *by George Brenton Laurie*—The Letters of an Officer of the Royal Irish Rifles on the Western Front During the Great War.

THE CAMELIERS *by Oliver Hogue*—A Classic Account of the Australians of the Imperial Camel Corps During the First World War in the Middle East.

RED DUST *by Donald Black*—A Classic Account of Australian Light Horsemen in Palestine During the First World War.

THE LEAN, BROWN MEN *by Angus Buchanan*—Experiences in East Africa During the Great War with the 25th Royal Fusiliers—the Legion of Frontiersmen.

THE NIGERIAN REGIMENT IN EAST AFRICA *by W. D. Downes*—On Campaign During the Great War 1916-1918.

THE 'DIE-HARDS' IN SIBERIA *by John Ward*—With the Middlesex Regiment Against the Bolsheviks 1918-19.

AVAILABLE ONLINE AT **www.leonaur.com**
AND FROM ALL GOOD BOOK STORES

ALSO FROM LEONAUR
AVAILABLE IN SOFTCOVER OR HARDCOVER WITH DUST JACKET

FARAWAY CAMPAIGN *by F. James*—Experiences of an Indian Army Cavalry Officer in Persia & Russia During the Great War.

REVOLT IN THE DESERT *by T. E. Lawrence*—An account of the experiences of one remarkable British officer's war from his own perspective.

MACHINE-GUN SQUADRON *by A. M. G.*—The 20th Machine Gunners from British Yeomanry Regiments in the Middle East Campaign of the First World War.

A GUNNER'S CRUSADE *by Antony Bluett*—The Campaign in the Desert, Palestine & Syria as Experienced by the Honourable Artillery Company During the Great War.

DESPATCH RIDER *by W. H. L. Watson*—The Experiences of a British Army Motorcycle Despatch Rider During the Opening Battles of the Great War in Europe.

TIGERS ALONG THE TIGRIS *by E. J. Thompson*—The Leicestershire Regiment in Mesopotamia During the First World War.

HEARTS & DRAGONS *by Charles R. M. F. Crutwell*—The 4th Royal Berkshire Regiment in France and Italy During the Great War, 1914-1918.

INFANTRY BRIGADE: 1914 *by John Ward*—The Diary of a Commander of the 15th Infantry Brigade, 5th Division, British Army, During the Retreat from Mons.

DOING OUR 'BIT' *by Ian Hay*—Two Classic Accounts of the Men of Kitchener's 'New Army' During the Great War including *The First 100,000* & *All In It*.

AN EYE IN THE STORM *by Arthur Ruhl*—An American War Correspondent's Experiences of the First World War from the Western Front to Gallipoli-and Beyond.

STAND & FALL *by Joe Cassells*—With the Middlesex Regiment Against the Bolsheviks 1918-19.

RIFLEMAN MACGILL'S WAR *by Patrick MacGill*—A Soldier of the London Irish During the Great War in Europe including *The Amateur Army*, *The Red Horizon* & *The Great Push*.

WITH THE GUNS *by C. A. Rose & Hugh Dalton*—Two First Hand Accounts of British Gunners at War in Europe During World War 1- Three Years in France with the Guns and With the British Guns in Italy.

THE BUSH WAR DOCTOR *by Robert V. Dolbey*—The Experiences of a British Army Doctor During the East African Campaign of the First World War.

AVAILABLE ONLINE AT **www.leonaur.com**
AND FROM ALL GOOD BOOK STORES

ALSO FROM LEONAUR
AVAILABLE IN SOFTCOVER OR HARDCOVER WITH DUST JACKET

THE 9TH—THE KING'S (LIVERPOOL REGIMENT) IN THE GREAT WAR 1914 - 1918 by Enos H. G. Roberts—Mersey to mud—war and Liverpool men.

THE GAMBARDIER by Mark Severn—The experiences of a battery of Heavy artillery on the Western Front during the First World War.

FROM MESSINES TO THIRD YPRES by Thomas Floyd—A personal account of the First World War on the Western front by a 2/5th Lancashire Fusilier.

THE IRISH GUARDS IN THE GREAT WAR - VOLUME 1 by Rudyard Kipling—Edited and Compiled from Their Diaries and Papers—The First Battalion.

THE IRISH GUARDS IN THE GREAT WAR - VOLUME 1 by Rudyard Kipling—Edited and Compiled from Their Diaries and Papers—The Second Battalion.

ARMOURED CARS IN EDEN by K. Roosevelt—An American President's son serving in Rolls Royce armoured cars with the British in Mesopotamia & with the American Artillery in France during the First World War.

CHASSEUR OF 1914 by Marcel Dupont—Experiences of the twilight of the French Light Cavalry by a young officer during the early battles of the great war in Europe.

TROOP HORSE & TRENCH by R.A. Lloyd—The experiences of a British Lifeguardsman of the household cavalry fighting on the western front during the First World War 1914-18.

THE EAST AFRICAN MOUNTED RIFLES by C.J. Wilson—Experiences of the campaign in the East African bush during the First World War.

THE LONG PATROL by George Berrie—A Novel of Light Horsemen from Gallipoli to the Palestine campaign of the First World War.

THE FIGHTING CAMELIERS by Frank Reid—The exploits of the Imperial Camel Corps in the desert and Palestine campaigns of the First World War.

STEEL CHARIOTS IN THE DESERT by S. C. Rolls—The first world war experiences of a Rolls Royce armoured car driver with the Duke of Westminster in Libya and in Arabia with T.E. Lawrence.

WITH THE IMPERIAL CAMEL CORPS IN THE GREAT WAR by Geoffrey Inchbald—The story of a serving officer with the British 2nd battalion against the Senussi and during the Palestine campaign.

AVAILABLE ONLINE AT **www.leonaur.com**
AND FROM ALL GOOD BOOK STORES

Lightning Source UK Ltd.
Milton Keynes UK
UKOW04f2112031217
313811UK00001B/11/P